To aid you in your activism, the worksheets in this book are available FREE on-line.

If you would like to download electronic versions of the worksheets, please visit

www.josseybass.com/go/onehouractivist

Thank you,
Christopher Kush

The
One-Hour
Activist

The One-Hour Activist

The 15 Most Powerful
Actions You Can Take
to Fight for the Issues and
Candidates You Care About

Christopher Kush

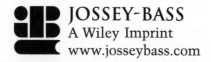

JOSSEY-BASS
A Wiley Imprint
www.josseybass.com

Published by Jossey-Bass
A Wiley Imprint
989 Market Street, San Francisco, CA 94103-1741   www.josseybass.com

ISBN: 0-7879-7300-9

Jossey-Bass books and products are available through most bookstores. To contact Jossey-Bass directly call our Customer Care Department within the U.S. at 800-956-7739, outside the U.S. at 317-572-3986 or fax 317-572-4002.

Jossey-Bass also publishes its books in a variety of electronic formats. Some content that appears in print may not be available in electronic books.

Library of Congress Cataloging-in-Publication Data

Kush, Christopher.
    The one-hour activist : the 15 most powerful actions you can take to fight for the issues and candidates you care about / Christopher Kush.—1st ed.
        p. cm.
    ISBN 0-7879-7300-9 (alk. paper)
    1. Political participation—United States. 2. Political activists—United States. I. Title.
JK1764.K84 2004
322.4'0973—dc22   2003023197

Printed in the United States of America
FIRST EDITION
PB Printing   10 9 8 7 6 5 4 3 2 1

CONTENTS

PREFACE

This is a tactical guide, not a civics class.

This is a book of action—a book you will put down to write, call, or meet with your elected officials or to engage in any of the twenty powerful grassroots actions explained in this book. These actions take you well beyond the voting booth and into the creation of substantive, influential dialogues with the people in power who represent you.

I understand that inspiration can be fleeting, so I have presented the core information you need to quickly and easily begin to have an impact on the issues you care about. This is a book with as little political theory and history as I could get away with. This is also a book you can grow with— and the deeper you explore *The One-Hour Activist,* the more sophisticated your actions will become.

Your first action to take, whatever your previous experience with politics is, should be to review exactly how grassroots advocacy works *and how it does not work*. This is the subject of the first chapter, Action 1. Americans harbor all sorts of misconceptions about the mechanics of grassroots advocacy, for example, that clicking on a prewritten e-mail is just as effective as a written letter because the only thing elected officials do with such communications is count them. In fact, some of the letters do get read, and the ones that do have a distinct advantage over those that are merely counted.

Take time to review the background information in Part One of this book—even if you just saw your representative saying something unconscionable on C-SPAN and you feel the need to immediately call or write her office. The initial chapters of this book form the foundation on which all of the subsequent grassroots actions depend.

The One-Hour Activist will help you understand what it is about a letter, or e-mail, or face-to-face meeting with a constituent that can influence the overall decision-making process in the offices of your lawmakers. Each action has a list of do's and don'ts. At the same time, I want you, the reader, to let go of white-knuckle adherence to mechanics in favor of more strategic considerations, like how you can individualize your letter, fax, or phone call to truly pique the interest of your elected officials. In any case, the primary rule of grassroots organizing is called "staying on message," which I define in Action 1.

Each chapter explores an individual grassroots action and contains a One-Hour Activist Rule that relates an important strategic consideration for you to keep in mind when engaging in that action. Each chapter also relates advice from the field, where an assortment of elected officials, journalists, lobbyists, and national organizers share an additional insight as an insider.

Worksheets are provided in chapters where I felt they would be helpful guiding your thinking or keeping track of individual information. Internet tips are provided in most chapters. Use these tips on the condition that you promise never to sign an on-line petition again without sending a more substantive message to your lawmakers. Illustrations abound for the visual learners out there. My aim was to make the book as friendly and as accessible as possible.

A few real-life stories and current legislative issues are used to provide examples of effective letters, telephone calls, and e-mails, but I have kept the use of current legislative issues to a minimum. The readers of this book will cut across the full American ideological spectrum, and I have attempted to avoid endorsing any particular party or ideology.

I do poke fun at the political process throughout the book to help de-mystify the process and to encourage your participation, so let yourself relax as you read.

Part One of the book contains the conceptual and analytical actions that you need to be an effective advocate, including how to determine what your issues really are, who represents you, how to join an organized interest group that may offer a grassroots network ready to add your voice in the fights related to your issues, what a legislative agenda is, how to an-alyze a bill, and how to conduct opposition research without sacrificing your integrity.

Part Two explains how to communicate with your elected officials in a persuasive manner. I cover all of the classics: writing a letter that matters, making an effective telephone call, and even that new classic: sending an e-mail that does not immediately get deleted as spam. I also include tips about how you can get others to join your cause and augment your efforts by en-couraging their participation.

After all that, I get to elections, which may seem a little counterintu-itive. It is not that elections are unimportant, but the focus here is to help you advance the specific issues you care about, which by definition must take you past Election Day and into the legislative process. I have begun with the most substantive one-hour actions you can take to have an impact on the actual laws that might or might not get passed. I assume that if you care enough about a particular issue, you already are an active voter—but that, to be honest, is not always a good assumption in our country, even among activists. I do provide some ideas as to how you can maximize your vote on Election Day, and it is in that chapter that I will encourage you to register and vote if you are not doing so already.

I also discuss the best ways to fork over cash to candidates—something that many Americans find off-putting about politics. That's a shame, be-cause until Congress passes dramatic campaign finance reform, being a campaign contributor is a powerful way to get access to your lawmakers. It remains your choice, and by the end of the chapter, you might very well choose to avail yourself of this option for getting yourself and the issues you care about recognized.

Part Four focuses on how to be an effective consumer of and contributor to the news media. I cover the basics like keeping a file of news clippings and then focus on how you can effectively communicate with the news media. Action 15 explains how to write a letter to the editor or an opinion editorial that has a chance of getting published.

Together, the first four parts of the book represent the basic one-hour actions you can take to fight for the issues you care about. Part Five presents five additional grassroots actions you can take. To be honest, these are actions that will take more than an hour to accomplish, but it is time well spent. These actions are more sophisticated and potentially more influential. Action 16, "Have a Face-to-Face Meeting with Your Representative," is about the most powerful grassroots action you can take as a concerned citizen, but it is not something that you can do in a single sitting in the privacy of your own home. Other skills that I describe are how to give public testimony, participate in a protest, volunteer for a local political campaign, and get on your local news by pitching stories and making yourself available for interviews. These actions provide a place for you to grow as an advocate as you become increasingly savvy about the political process and increasingly knowledgeable with the substantive details surrounding the issues you care about.

I wish you the best of luck discovering your issues, fighting for them, and coordinating your efforts with other like-minded individuals to have an impact on our government at the federal, state, and local levels. Our democracy is never so strong as when a lot of people, from a lot of different walks of life, with a lot of different viewpoints, all clamor over a single piece of legislation.

Cacophony signals health, not dysfunction, in a democracy. I encourage you to contribute to this noise but with a sense of perspective. Try not to characterize every legislative occurrence as any bigger a step toward true peace, freedom, justice, equality, and prosperity than it inevitably really is— tentative, piecemeal, stopgap, and fully rooted in sensible hope.

We live in a dangerous time, where people with deeply held beliefs increasingly sanction violence as a valid form of political expression. If our democracy depends on your participation, it also relies on your restraint. Dialogue is not possible if we nurture a belief that success can be characterized only by the annihilation of our opposition. Perhaps as you struggle to find your voice, you will also endeavor to be amused more than angered by a democracy that changes slowly and imperfectly in response to your efforts.

February 2004

Christopher Kush
Washington, D.C.

For my mother, who was not an especially political person but loved books

ACKNOWLEDGMENTS

With thanks and gratitude to all of those people who assisted with the creation of this book:

For writers, advocacy begins with the agent, and I want to thank Jeffrey Kleinman at Graybill & English in Washington, D.C., for championing the cause. From there the struggle moves to the editor who has to fight for the book at the publishing house before it ever has a chance to compete in a bookstore. Special thanks to my editor at Jossey-Bass, Johanna Vondeling, who nurtured this project as a valuable approach to a subject that been grasped at but never fully captured.

Thanks to Allsion Brunner for editorial assistance and Andrea Reider for the wonderful book design.

Any errors or omissions are my own, but there are many who assisted with this book, and I would like to recognize their contributions. Angela Taylor helped develop material for this book through successive drafts and workshops. Jean-Michel Brevelle conducted research, interviews, and assistance on the initial draft. Anita Douglas provided technical assistance and coordinated the input of our contributors. Pat Scully helped copyedit the manuscript and provided valuable feedback at a critical juncture.

Thanks so very much to the advocates who generously allowed me to use their personal stories in this book by way of inspiration and example to the reader: Lisa Bayha, Shelby Wilbourn, and Colleen Stack.

Several elected officials agreed to be interviewed for this book to give activists a player's view of the legislative process. I especially thank Representative Jessie Jackson Jr. for patiently answering numerous questions between critical House votes. I also thank Representative Steny Hoyer and Lawrence Pacheco, press secretary and legislative assistant to Representative Mark Udall.

Several state representatives shared their time and expertise for this project including Delegate Luis Simmons, Delegate Sandy Rosenberg, and Delegate Rich Maldonado of the Maryland State Assembly.

I am indebted to the lobbyists who helped provide alternative tips and insights that give the material more depth than I alone could provide and to their respective organizations, especially Jane Weirich (American Cancer Society), Michael Crawford (Human Rights Campaign), Justin Moore (American Physical Therapy Association), Grayson Fowler (Campaign for Tobacco-Free Kids), W. Minor Carter (Van Scoyoc Associates), Carlea Bauman (American Diabetes Association), Stephanie Vance (AdVanced Consulting), John Goodwin (Humane Society of the United States), Ryan Clary (Project Inform), Peter Larson, (Metro Teen AIDS), Bob Ensinger (Paralyzed Veterans of America), Karl Moeller (American Heart Association), Pete Sepp (National Taxpayers Union), Frank Ryan (American Dental Association), Randy Rutta (Easter Seals), and William C. Miller Jr. (U.S. Chamber of Commerce).

Finally, thanks to the reporters and newspaper editors who took time out of their hectic schedules to provide advice: Kevin Schultze (WJLA-Washington, D.C.), Nancy Wiener (ABC News, Washington, D.C.), Dana Kozlov (WBBM-TV, Chicago), Katie Shaver (*Washington Post*), and Jo-Ann Armao (*Washington Post*).

Finally, this being my third book on grassroots organizing, I'd like to recognize some of my original mentors and colleagues who helped encourage me or struggled by my side in the beginning—in particular, Bill Skeen, Phill Wilson, Mario Solis Marich, Mark Etzel, Pat Acosta, Matt Patrick, Grayson Fowler, John Mortimer, Alan LoFaso, Sophia Kwong, Bill Givens, Howard Jacobs, Troy Fernandez, Paul Daniels, Jean-Michel Brevelle, Connie Norman, and Cornelius Baker. Thank you.

THE AUTHOR

Christopher Kush has trained thousands of citizens from all over the United States to effectively influence Congress as well as state and local governments. As president of Soapbox Consulting, he has helped design Lobby Days, grassroots campaigns, and training seminars for many national organizations, including the American Heart Association, American Cancer Society, Girl Scouts of the USA, American Psychological Association, Easter Seals, and Arthritis Foundation. He lives in Washington, D.C. He can be contacted through www.soapboxconsulting.com.

Never doubt that a small group of thoughtful committed citizens can change the world. Indeed it's the only thing that ever has.

—MARGARET MEAD

Each snowflake in an avalanche pleads not guilty.

—STANISLAW J. LEC

Democracy in Action

Why is it that any discussion about our system of government requires reverent and grave tones somewhere between a graduate dissertation and remembering the dead? Discussing American democracy always seems so, I don't know, serious. In this regard, it has a lot in common with sex education: if you sat in on a high school class dealing with the subject, you'd be convinced it wasn't any fun.

I recently watched a documentary on the U.S. Capitol where otherwise serious historians and battle-hardened journalists felt inclined to treacly veneration and, worse, childlike amusement as if the Capitol was wonderfully fun, and impishly surprising, and well . . . harmless—as if these experts were not aware that our Congress met there.

You sometimes hear the Capitol referred to majestically as "The People's House," with suggestions that inside the Capitol, the work of "The People" gets done—perhaps not as efficiently as might be hoped, but in the long run in our best interests and occasionally with some fantastic oratory ringing off the walls. Let's face it, for any given action in the Capitol while some of "The People" may feel that their work is being done, others will feel that they are getting done in.

Architecturally, the Capitol is a grand structure in a lots-of-white-marble sort of way. The ceilings are far more colorful than you might expect. There are statues to look at. A beautiful rotunda. And the mazelike hallways and staircases perhaps beckon every American child to come in, explore, get lost in their Capitol—The People's House.

I guess this is all innocent enough—except for one thing. As anyone who has been to the U.S. Capitol can tell you, particularly after the September 11, 2001, terrorist attacks: the Capitol doesn't really feel like *your house*. Even the most casual stroll through the interior, which is now strictly limited to citizens on official tours or with official passes, raises some obvious questions.

For one thing, who are all of the people with guns? Did someone invite them over? Ah, security, we are told; it's now necessary. Okay, but what about exploring the mazelike hallways? It is immediately clear that the Capitol, that most central site in our most open and representative government, is characterized as much by places you, as a citizen, are not allowed to explore, as by the beautiful frescoes that illuminate the ceilings. *No unescorted visitors beyond this point* signs abound, as well as frequent admonishments against taking photographs or video.

And should you miss a sign, perhaps because you innocently begin to wander through "The People's House," there is an abundance of those guests with guns posted to keep you on the official tour or point you toward the exits.

We, The People, are not allowed on the Floor of the House or Senate chambers where representatives and senators debate, vote, and otherwise officially conduct the day's business. You can, however, if you have a special pass, climb to the top of the Capitol chambers and watch the proceedings of the House and Senate from the galleries, after first surrendering all of your electronic equipment and passing through yet another metal detector. You are not allowed to read or take notes while you are there.

Welcome home, America.

The inescapable reality to even the most disinterested tourist is that the U.S. Capitol is a high-security, formal, byzantine game board where the distribution and exercise of political power take place in our country. This is real power—the power to commandeer your wages in the form of taxes, the power to declare war against another country, the power to attract the attention of the news media, the power to oppose or even impeach the president, the power to guide our freedoms in the form of laws. And the exercise of this power involves conflicts—major conflicts between ideologies, political parties, egos, and money. How this power is disbursed and how it is controlled is the genius of our remarkable system of government, but this is not necessarily an inviting place.

You are allowed—not compelled but allowed—to participate in this contentious mess if you want to. Why should you want to get involved? Because, honestly, once you get going, it's a lot more fun than the official tour. Because the U.S. Senate recently designated April 21 through 27, 2003, as National Cowboy Poetry Week, "to recognize the importance of cowboy poetry for future generations." And, most important, because if you don't become involved, you may not be considered one of "The People" that "The People's House" represents.

ISN'T MONEY THE ONLY THING THAT MATTERS?

To understand how an everyday citizen can have an impact on our government takes some effort in a world where few of us have the energy or time to indulge in new pursuits. We have a complicated system of government that represents a complicated country. Sensing that, there are those among us who believe that the easiest way to deal with our government is to dismiss it out of hand by displaying all of the negative emotions, declaring, "Everyone else can be led around like sheep, but I know what is really going on, and I'm not going to waste one second on it." The reality is usually that the average disgruntled citizen has no idea who his or her federal, state, and local representatives are, much less what they are really up to.

There are others who suspect that money—big money, more money than they have anyway—is what really determines the course of government and that most of us are left out of the process. This is a serious concern, and not entirely without basis. It is a well-documented fact that some very big business interests invest lots of money during elections on candidates for public office, and after elections, they spend millions more on lobbyists and communications consultants because these interests have business before our federal and state legislatures.

How awful for the average American who does not, say, have controlling interest in a Fortune 500 company, and who does not receive dividends every quarter in part influenced by what lobbyists can secure, to be left out of a supposedly fair and open system of government in the United States.

And yet. And yet. If you pay close attention in the state legislatures and in Congress, you will occasionally hear grousing from those very industries: they do not always get everything they want despite all of those campaign donations and all of those retainers. Now how does *that* happen?

Here's one recent example. Maryland is bordered by other states that in recent years have relaxed their gambling laws to allow slot machines—and Maryland, like any other state, finds that it sometimes could use a little more revenue (or a lot more, depending on the year). Meanwhile, Maryland has had to endure the crowing of nearby New Jersey, West Virginia, and Delaware, all generating millions of extra dollars in tax revenue from slot machines. Maryland's historic concession to gaming, the horse racing industry, claims it is on the verge of collapse, in part because those in charge of Maryland's racetracks say they are no longer able to compete with the gambling options available within easy driving distance.

Indeed, there are a number of Marylanders who sympathize with the plight of the racetracks or are enticed by promises that public schools would be the primary beneficiaries of increased state revenues if slot machines were made legal in the state. Other Marylanders are resolutely opposed—including the former Democratic governor who was term-limited out of office in 2002 and replaced by a Republican who campaigned on a pro-slots platform and won.

Maryland experienced a change in leadership at the state level, public opinion was divided, the racetracks were crying for relief, the schools needed money, and the gambling industry was aware that slot machines could generate millions of dollars in revenue, even after the state took its cut. In politics, this is what we call low-hanging fruit, and accordingly, in 2003, the gambling industry spent at least $1.5 million to help pass a bill through the Maryland state legislature for the new governor to sign that would legalize slot machines in the state.

There was, of course, opposition. There is *always* opposition in America. Corporate America is not generally surprised that there is opposition. It just outspends them. In this case, the gambling industry outspent their opposition at least fifty to one, because when you looked at a business plan, $1.5 million was a drop in the bucket compared with what the industry stood to gain.

Now we get to the part that is a little hard to believe. It may even seem a bit outrageous believing what we do about how money systemically corrupts our system of government.

The gambling industry lost, despite terrific odds and a whole lot of money.

It did not lose because one angry citizen wrote one angry letter. It lost for a number of reasons, in part related to the political infighting between the new governor and the state legislature. But there was also a nascent grassroots effort to be reckoned with. It was not well funded, but it was visible and able to effectively and compellingly demonstrate that a significant number of Maryland voters were truly and thoughtfully opposed to slot machines.

Several things are instructive from this example. *The opposition was active.* The opposition did not abandon their elected officials to weigh the pros and cons without their input. *The opposition did not need millions of dollars to access their elected officials or get the attention of the news media.* In some cases their elected officials came to them. The gambling industry's money may have guaranteed a hearing in the state legislature, but it did not in any way silence the voice of those who chose to speak up against slot machines. *It is not over yet.* Issues like these tend not to be resolved—ever. The gambling industry will probably try to legalize slots during the next legislative session and again the session after that. By that time, perhaps the grassroots opposition will have time to professionalize, do some fundraising of its own, and establish an ongoing effort to fight gambling interests in the state. On the other hand, maybe it will not. If the opposition retires after its recent victory, it will lose the long-term war despite winning the opening battle.

THE ONE-HOUR ACTIVIST

People can and do regularly have an impact on our system of government, even against well-funded interests. Many people are surprised to discover the attention that lawmakers will give to a thoughtful letter or conversation that provides insight into the district or the voters who live there. There is a tremendous amount of influence we can choose to exert in our democracy beyond our vote on Election Day.

So where do you come in? How can you use your voice to make government respond to the issues that are personally important to you? How do you get your legislators to consider your opinion and include your stories in the ongoing debate?

Americans who are not professional lobbyists generally spend eight (or more) hours a day being exhausted and irritated by their jobs with all of the concomitant crises they entail. After work, there are families to attend to, personal lives, even hobbies other than politics.

And why shouldn't there be? One of the unsung advantages of American democracy is that our elected officials are given the responsibility of attending to all public matters—with or without our attention, with or without our participation, with or without our input. A government that needed to be constantly and extravagantly attended to by its citizens would be a different sort of tyranny than subjugation to a dictator but tyranny nonetheless.

Meanwhile, the Internet, computers, automated phone banks, and all of the other new communications technology promise a return to civic engagement by presenting grassroots advocacy as unimaginably simple and quick—your entire contribution to environmental battles in the time it takes to click a mouse button. It is a promise that has begun to falter. Unfortunately, on-line petitions and prewritten e-mail messages, while relatively easy to send, reek of being impersonal, and personal stories have always been, and remain, the foundation of grassroots influence.

Still, millions of Americans every year are prodded by political groups asking them to engage in instant grassroots tasks on-line. The problem with this approach to the average well-meaning but stressed-out American is that being asked to perform a rote exercise, like copying a sample letter, can seem a little silly. The question arises: If my letter is not individual in any way, why do I have to be the one who writes it? I'm busy here! Legislative offices are likely to express a similar sort of frustration when they receive these cookie-cutter communications that contain no unique information from the sender.

Grassroots organizers often say that advocates must perform these little grassroots actions so that they can be counted. "Being counted" is often assumed to be the most important aspect of grassroots advocacy. Well, maybe on Election Day.

Asking Americans to do less is not necessarily an effective way to overcome the time constraints we face. Jumping through silly hoops does not make us feel energized or involved so much as aware that we do not have a lot of time to be jumping through silly hoops—especially when our lawmakers, on receipt of a bunch of instant, identical communications, are less and less convinced that the constituents clicking that mouse really understand the issue, are following it closely, have anything important to add to the discussion, or will be aware come election time how the member actually voted on it.

The One-Hour Activist presents an approach to grassroots advocacy that brings you into the corridors of power in a meaningful way—to be a player, not a glorified copying machine. This approach ensures that if you spend an hour commenting on a particular piece of legislation, you are actually communicating with elected officials rather than making copies of sample letters. To do this, you need to put the idea of instant communication with your elected officials out of your mind. You've got to dedicate more than a few seconds on-line to fighting for the issues you care about.

The good news is that a more substantive and more powerful dialogue with your elected officials does not require that you devote your entire existence and every free minute you have to politics. Advocacy *can* be a reasonable pursuit.

Advocates and grassroots organizers alike can rethink how we as citizens interact with our government. We should change from nameless, faceless drones who sign postcards or e-mail petitions in monolithic fashion to informed individuals who establish professional relationships with our elected officials that foster a deeper understanding of how the issues we care about affect our lives: real people living in real places. You deserve that much for your participation.

"THE PEOPLE'S HOUSE" REVISITED?

Every action detailed in this book was chosen with an abiding respect for the intelligence and experiences that Americans have accrued through their personal and professional lives. The skills that follow are truly powerful. They present an opportunity for you to meaningfully enter the playing field of American politics. *The One-Hour Activist* also represents a challenge to every elected official in this country: the challenge that "The People's House" and every other legislative body in this country should have its openness, its efficiency, and its promise judged not by how freely Americans are allowed to physically roam the marble-lined corridors of power but by how broad and inclusive a cross-section of the country is reflected in the dialogue at every level of government in the United States.

The One-Hour Activist

PART 1

Gather Information and Strategize

Learn How Grassroots Advocacy Works

In this chapter, you will learn:

- How grassroots advocacy works
- Why voting is not enough to win on your issues
- Why where you live determines your political strategy
- Eight important grassroots concepts
- What "staying on message" means and why it is imperative

Our government is extraordinarily fragmented for reasons that you probably cherish. Putting lots of people from lots of different districts in charge of our government seems to have been an effective way to guard against too much power being concentrated in the hands of any one individual.

Our government has ingeniously avoided this problem for a couple of hundred years by fracturing power into an almost indefensible number of little pieces. We may have a president of the United States, but the president must rely on Congress to pass laws. And what does the Congress consist of? A couple of close confidants? No. A committee of ten expert advisers? No. A couple dozen of the richest or smartest people in the land? No. The Congress currently consists of 535 publicly elected officials who, more or less like the president, feel that they are to some extent in charge of the governance of our country. The Congress is divided into two chambers: the House of Representatives (435) and the Senate (100). The executive and legislative branches of our federal government are in turn kept in check by the Supreme Court, yet another body with an assortment of powers.

And that's just the federal government. You probably have a state government that is organized in a similar, highly fragmented fashion. Then there's a local or city government that also governs you. If it sounds hopelessly convoluted, you are beginning to get the idea.

Our country has the sort of organizational chart that would mar any CEO's sleep with fitful starts, yet your freedoms depend on this arrangement. The inherent confusion of the American system of government helps deter our elected officials from the evil expressions of power that a more efficient system of government would facilitate.

All of these little pieces of power are divided up into legislative districts according to geography, and the registered voters who live in each district generally get to elect their representatives. This seems a fair way to divide influence, but it has another benefit. So many people from so many different places get elected to run our country that a broad number of stakeholders—not just people from different political parties—but people from far-flung places with different economies, different experiences, different lives—are potentially involved in the governance of our country. In addition to their own differences being brought to bear on the questions of the day, our representatives risk losing their power on Election Day if they do not satisfactorily reflect the needs, goals, and ideas of the different groups that live within the different districts they represent.

In practice, the structure of our government results in a number of frustrations. First, the need for compromise is beyond question in U.S. politics because there are too many stakeholders affected by any proposed law to keep it pure. Another drawback is that resolving the various conflicts created by a multitude of interested parties can make the actual process of crafting legislation convoluted and time-consuming. You probably already knew that. Some lament this, but a government characterized by the unan-

Illustration 1.1. The Federal Legislative Process and the Role of Constituents

Constituents play a critical role in the legislative process by acting as a conduit of information between elected officials and their home districts.

Things That Influence Lawmakers:

- Campaign Contributions
- Political Parties
- Other Lawmakers
- The News Media
- Scholars and Researchers
- Their Life Experiences
- Institutional Support (e.g., the Congressional Budget Office and the General Accounting Office)
- Personal Staff
- Community-based Advocates
- Re-election Campaign Strategy

- Statistics from the district
- Real-life examples
- Issue expertise
- Access to district voters
- News media opportunities

imous embrace of extraordinarily simple solutions to public problems is called a dictatorship, and you do not want that.

If passing legislation in this country were quick and straightforward, ice cream would have been outlawed long ago—and there would be even more serious curbing of our freedoms. I can't think of any just now, but that ice cream report was pretty scary.

In the end, the structure protects us, but it does not guarantee that the actual governance will be high quality. Our government merely offers promise. Actual governance is left up to those in power and those who choose to participate in the process (see Illustration 1.1).

THE GRASSROOTS STAR OF INFLUENCE

There are five main reasons that an elected official would want to do your bidding: voting, contributing, volunteering, visibility, and communication. These five characteristics form the grassroots star of influence (see Illustration 1.2).

• Voting. This is the most important and most basic of the reasons that an elected official would want to pay attention to you. In most cases, being a constituent obviates the need for a lengthy or technical discussion or debate related to your issues. It is not that your legislators are not interested in the substantive provisions in any piece of legislation, but they usually have staff who can help them understand what a bill might do. What your legislator does not know is if any particular piece of legislation is a priority to her voters—a priority for passage and a priority for the limited amount of funding that the government can provide. If you say a bill is a priority and you are a voter, then it becomes a priority. No amount of campaign funding can supplant the power you have as a voter to help determine the legislative priorities for your district. (See Part Three.)

• Contributing. In addition to votes, it takes a lot of money for elected officials to run for office and then to run for reelection, and there is no indi-

Illustration 1.2. The Grassroots Star of Influence

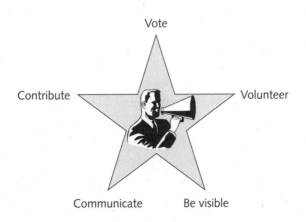

Vote

Contribute

Volunteer

Communicate

Be visible

cation that things are going to change anytime soon. This means that elected officials must constantly be chasing campaign contributions—and the easiest way for them to do that is by keeping the people who have already given them money happy. If you are a campaign contributor, you are important to your elected officials. (See Part Three.)

• Volunteering. A third way to get the ear of a current or potential legislator is to volunteer for a candidate's campaign. Labor is very expensive, and most electoral campaigns are starved for cash. That means that people who volunteer often become part of a close, extremely valued circle of supporters who do the heavy day-to-day lifting of putting (or keeping) a candidate in office. Volunteers are seldom forgotten. (See Part Five.)

• Visibility. Elected officials are sometimes attracted to people with high visibility. People who are highly visible often represent or influence their own constituency of voters and contributors as opinion leaders in their communities. If the president of the local university, for example, is vocal in her support of the governor, that support might generate a large number of votes for the governor. The governor would do well to learn the issues and positions that are important to the president of the university. (See Part Four.)

One-Hour Rule

Grassroots success relies on three things: where you live, how you communicate, and if people in other districts are asking for the same thing.

• Communication. If you are a voter, a campaign contributor, a volunteer, or a community leader, then your elected officials want to make you happy, but they cannot read your mind. They depend on you to communicate your general areas of interest on the campaign trail and to substantively inform them about specific legislation when they are in office. Many people assume that legislators are interested in counting letters or phone calls related to an issue and do not really care to delve into individual stories or arguments. This is not true. Elected officials need anecdotal, local stories to make the statistics related to a particular initiative come alive. Local arguments and stories are both welcome, even sought after, by elected officials. Such communications form the backbone of high-quality grassroots actions as opposed to low-quality actions (like preprinted postcards and petitions) that focus being counted in a legislative office without attempting to establish a substantive exchange with your lawmakers.

WELCOME TO THE GRASSROOTS DRIVE-IN

Cultivating an ongoing relationship with your elected officials is the best way to serve the issues you care about over the long term, but your efforts alone do not determine grassroots success. Ultimately, your efforts must be mirrored by advocates across a large number of districts in order to have a federal, state, or local government pass the bills you care about.

This is how it works. Picture your larger struggle for success as a trip to the Grassroots Drive-In, where the feature film is *The Grassroots Success Story.*

You want as many elected officials as possible to see this movie, and you have a little two-seater convertible. But you've got only one extra seat in your convertible, so you can invite one and only one lawmaker to come to the drive-in with you. No matter how hard you try (and don't even think about the trunk), you can bring one and only one representative in with you. Once inside the drive-in, your lovely convertible will take up one and only one parking space. (This scenario is sketched out in Illustration 1.3.)

The problem is that *The Grassroots Success Story* will not be shown until at least half of the parking spots are filled. You take up only one spot in the parking lot. How do you get the other available parking spots filled with legislators? Other people with other two-seater convertibles have to con-vince their legislators to come to the drive-in in their cars until enough of the parking spots are filled.

The reason you have a two-seater convertible is that for almost every leg-islative battle, you will have one and only one elected official who represents

Illustration 1.3. Welcome to the Grassroots Drive-In

You have a two-seater convertible and a ticket to the Grassroots Drive-in.

You must convince your own representative to see the show with you.

The movie will not start until at least half of the parking spots are full. You must work in concert with constituents from other districts to get lawmakers to the drive-in (and move your issue forward).

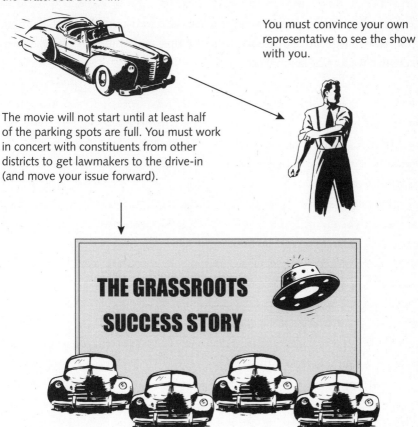

your interests. (You have two legislators in the U.S. Senate, but let's keep it simple for now.) No matter how hard you try, it is almost impossible to make any elected official other than the one who officially represents you care about your requests. This is both an advantage and a disadvantage. The advantage is that you are the key to bringing your elected official to the Grassroots Drive-In. No one who lives outside the district will be more persuasive than you. The disadvantage is that you must rely on advocates from other districts to convince their own legislators to vote your way.

Each parking space at the drive-in stands for a single district represented by an individual legislator. More than half of the spaces need to be filled for the movie to begin because a majority vote at any level of government is generally required to advance legislation. Efforts must be coordinated for the grassroots to have a real impact on the fate of a particular piece of legislation.

It is important to understand that each convertible does not represent a single letter, or phone call, or e-mail. What if you are fighting for an issue that generates 100,000 letters? If those 100,000 are all from people living in the same district, then they are all sharing one little convertible. Their 100,000 letters might very well bring only one representative to the drive-in—and the movie will not be screened. If, however, those 100,000 letters are from 250 different districts, and if those letters are sufficiently compelling, then you might get 250 legislators to the movie; the trailers will roll and you can treat your lawmakers to popcorn.

Note that it does not necessarily take more than one person to cultivate a representative's vote on a given issue. It is the rare issue that generates bags of mail in a legislative office, and one compelling local story can secure the support of your federal or state lawmakers, but you must engage in high-quality grassroots actions to have this sort of impact. You must provide local, individual information when you communicate for your elected officials. If you send cookie-cutter letters and e-mail to a legislative office that are not personalized in any way, they will simply be counted. Such low-quality grassroots actions require many more advocates to secure a lawmaker's support.

A high-quality grassroots advocate can influence her legislators, but that is not enough to secure a victory in Congress or the state legislature. The only way we can exert some influence on the entire system is by coordinating our efforts with others from other districts. Advocates for any issue must be heard from the broadest possible geographical region, but each advocate needs to concentrate on his or her own representatives, preferably with the high-quality grassroots actions outlined in this book.

EIGHT IMPORTANT GRASSROOTS CONCEPTS

Here are some additional concepts for you to keep in mind when you get started as an advocate.

1: Voting Is Not Enough

The devil is in the details, and once you have elected a candidate to office, that person will have to deal with those details as they relate to the issues you care about. When candidates are campaigning, they tend to advertise their issue

Advice from the Field

The Honorable Jesse Jackson Jr.

Member

U.S. House of Representatives (Illinois, Second District)

"Advocates need to commit to a system of belief. You want to set a fixed star that is nearly unobtainable. This will steer you through any particular bill in Congress, through any setbacks; you won't burn out; you won't be tempted to turn on others who are fighting for the same cause. Your advocacy will be sustainable over the long run."

positions in broad strokes. They are for the right to abortion or against it. They are for gun control or against it. They are for gay and lesbian rights or against them. Legislation, however, is specific, and the legislation that is introduced in any given legislative session will address your issues in a specific way. Along the way there will be trade-offs, amendments, deals—that is, politics. If you abandon your issue after Election Day, anything might happen.

2: Geography Is the Single Most Important Thing About You and Your Issues

It does not matter if you have figured out how to send an e-mail to every member of Congress. It does not matter if you have honed a razor-sharp set of arguments that you believe will compel even the most intractable of elected officials to come around to your way to thinking. The single most important thing about you when you initiate communication with an elected official is not who you are, or what your job title is, or how well you can argue. It is where you live. Period. If you live in the district, your elected officials want to make you happy. If you don't live in the district but you've got a great argument, they probably do not care. In the political arena, a district mailing address trumps a strong argument from a nonconstituent every time.

In my job, I set up a lot of meetings between elected officials and constituents. It is not uncommon for someone to come to Washington, D.C., believing that he should be able to see anyone he wants—as if everyone represents him. Usually he also believes that what elected officials crave are thick folders brimming with lots of good information. Neither of these beliefs is true. The only information an elected official is generally looking for is that an actual voter supports a specific bill. There is no need for extensive argument or debate. Officials crave votes, and if you cannot deliver a vote, any fantastic arguments you may have suddenly pale. A debate with a constituent from a different district usually annoys rather than enlightens.

3: One Angry Letter Does Not Change the World

There is an assumption among some advocates that their elected officials are slightly dim, morally compromised, and in need of scolding into doing the right thing. Whether on paper or in person, these advocates generally start out loud and angry, and they end with an abrupt list of demands. This is not the way to win friends and influence people.

Equally unfortunate is an expectation that one indignant e-mail should bring the whole of the U.S. Congress to a grinding halt. As a rule, U.S. senators are harder to scare than that.

Yes, I hope you find your voice, and I hope you use it. But remember that you are one of hundreds of thousands of citizens in any legislative district with a lot of occupations, outlooks, and concerns. There are a lot of people with legitimate viewpoints that are different from yours. In this book, I will do my best to give you the tools and the confidence you need to interact with your elected officials in a powerful and persuasive way— but a little humility is appropriate.

At the same time, you should not feel that if your letter does not convince everyone in Congress to vote your way that you are a failure. You may convince your particular representative to appreciate your views on a specific issue, but he or she is but one of many. Remember the Grassroots Drive-In: for the grassroots to win, many people who care about the same things you do but live in different legislative districts must communicate with their representatives. You play an important role in that process because you have the opportunity to compel your representative's vote with compelling local stories and arguments.

Your job, however, is necessarily limited to your specific representatives— not your entire state legislature, the entire Congress, or the world.

4: Instant Grassroots (Like Signing On-Line Petitions) Is Not Especially Effective

Elected officials are perfectly aware that the postcard you signed at the grocery store took all of about ten seconds of your time. They know that you don't really understand the issue. They might suspect that even though you signed the postcard, you don't really care. Elected officials try their hardest to insist that they respond to every piece of communication in their office the same way, but the fact is that most are aware of just how much effort each piece of communication takes the sender. Ridiculously simple grassroots methods are discounted accordingly. But letters that are personalized with stories and statistics from the district generally have more of an impact than constituents assume.

5: Money Is Part of the Game

The one exception to geography that elected officials are likely to grant is to campaign contributors—those people who donate money to their political campaigns. You may not like the fact that money plays a role in American politics, but it is part of the game. If you refuse to take out your checkbook the same way you write letters or vote, you should know that you are taking an effective weapon out of your arsenal, especially because modest donations can and do get the attention of elected officials. You can, of course, choose to wage your battle on other fronts—that is your choice—but that choice just might abandon a powerful tool to your opposition.

Sometimes advocates feel that they cannot possibly compete with the amounts of money thrown around by big business interests and so decide not to contribute to political campaigns. This is a shame because even a modest campaign contribution is likely to get the attention of your elected officials. (See Action 13.)

6: Elected Officials Are Real People—With All of the Complexity and Imperfection That Implies

Because so many people are involved in the job of governance in our country, Americans are always guaranteed that there is a wide range of personality types in office. The only way you can discover if you are represented ably is to write, call, or meet with your elected officials once in a while. It's the political equivalent of looking under the bed.

When you begin fighting for your issues, make sure you focus on the actual individuals who are elected to represent you—and really try to understand them. Your understanding of the legislative process, parliamentary procedure, and legislative maneuvers is of secondary importance to your understanding of the individual personalities that belong to your actual representatives.

7: One Successful Grassroots Campaign Will Not Settle Your Issues Once and for All

The second you were able to secure an equal high-quality education for every American child, some group would explode in angry opposition based on the most tenuous research that chalk dust in public schools was dangerous to children and that the entire system had to be dismantled.

But before the system could be dismantled, another group of people would want to divert the funding because the quality education would seem to be costing too much, meaning that it was costing *something*. Let's face it: the chalk alone to supply every classroom, to educate every kid in the country, would look like a shocking figure when it was all added up.

And other groups would spring up, with other complaints, other ambitions, other agendas, other uses for the funding. So settle in and get comfortable. The fights over the issues that you care about are going to be ongoing, long-term battles that precede your involvement and continue long after you have burned out emotionally, intellectually, or physically. Health care will always be an issue. Education will always be an issue. Civil rights will always be an issue. Terrorism and "homeland security" will now always be an issue.

8: "Staying on Message" Is the Ultimate Law of Grassroots Activism

Staying on message is serious business to grassroots organizers. Although every advocate has his or her own story, own experiences, own personal voice on the issues of the day, the grassroots will only be as effective as it is able to have everyone who cares about a given issue make the *same exact request*— no matter how individualized their justification for that request is.

You can work alone, identify your own issues, write your own letters. Your issues will benefit in some small way from your participation. But if you want your government to respond, you should consider working in conjunction with others who care about the same issues that you do. In most cases, this coordination is achieved through a grassroots network run by an interest group. (See Action 4 to find out how to join an existing grassroots network that fights for the issues you care about.)

In either case, it takes a lot of people, from a lot of different places, making the same request, to seize the attention of our elected officials on a single, specific issue. For real change, this process of coordinating a broad coalition of advocates to share their personal stories and local arguments while making the same request must be repeated over and over again at every level of government. Only then will a sufficient amount of legislation be enacted to effectively address a given issue.

Pick Your Issues and Your Angle

In this chapter, you will learn:

- Experiences that might help transform you into an advocate
- Your choice between using formal arguments or personal stories when communicating with lawmakers
- Five conversations that your elected officials want to have with you
- Elements of a powerful personal story

Most Americans do not become politically active because they value civic participation. Perhaps some Americans vote because they feel they should, but advocacy usually requires a more urgent impulse. Americans tend to become activists when they are (often unexpectedly) affected by an issue. That means most of us are single-issue advocates.

You wake up one morning and discover you care, for maybe the first time in your life, about what the government is doing, is not doing, or might be doing. You might join an organization because you have a casual interest in some issue area and they ask you to become part of something they call an action network. Maybe a friend sends you an e-mail asking you to sign a petition.

Before you realize what you have gotten yourself into, you get your first Action Alert in the mail telling you to write a letter to your representative (Chapter Four explains Action Alerts). This is perhaps the first time you have ever considered communicating with an elected official. Determined to contribute to the struggle, you sit down to write. For overall tone, you opt to sound like a combination lawyer, debate team captain, statistician, and lobbyist. You will be indignant, condescending, suspicious, and positively dazzling with the force of your reason. This is a common impulse but not a very auspicious beginning.

One-Hour Rule

Your life, your professional expertise, and your local experiences provide you with almost everything you need to know to fight for the issues you care about— no matter what specific request you make.

Your most fundamental challenge when you wake up transformed into an advocate is to remain human—not just because it is easier than pretending to be something you are not, but because it is the most compelling contribution you can make to support the issues you care about. If done right, you can sometimes dwarf the influence of the lobbyists, lawyers, and statisticians with the pure unadulterated force of . . . you.

TO ARGUE OR TO SHARE, THAT IS THE QUESTION

You have to make a choice when you personally lobby your elected officials: you can either formally argue your point, or you can share your individual story—and by that I mean, explain why the issue matters to you as a voter from the district. When most of us think of advocacy, we think of engaging in a formal, statistics-laden debate with an elected official. Indeed, organized interest groups are known for providing their grassroots advocates with bulleted lists of "talking points" on specific issues that seem to encourage this approach. Sometimes advocates take this approach because it just sounds like lobbying. At the same time, lobbyists do not generally have access to local stories and experiences related to the specific district of any particular lawmaker. Advocates do. If you use your personal knowledge correctly, you can make your elected officials connect through the heart rather than the head, and that commitment tends to be more lasting.

Our governments are absolutely drowning in statistics. One million, one billion, one trillion. On Capitol Hill these are very prevalent numbers. Elected officials quickly become inoculated against such numbers, but advocates seem to remain enchanted. Nothing makes us more comfortable when supporting a particular bill than being able to brandish some impressive statistic, preferably in the millions. The only problem is that large numbers alone usually fail to impress.

Lawmakers usually have all of the impressive statistics that they need at their fingertips. What they don't have, and what only constituents can provide, is a way to make the statistics come alive. You can make these statistics dance, but only if you put the large statistics out of your mind and get down to the number one. There is no shortage of lobbyists who will identify, analyze, and track legislation, but the arguments that lobbyists make are usually far more sweeping than the viewpoint that an individual constituent can provide. Without real-life examples, there is no way for lawmakers, their staff, or the news media to make sense of the impressive numbers that flood our capitals.

There are five conversations that legislators really want to have with their constituents. They are set out in Illustration 2.1.

A lawmaker will fight determinedly to fund research for a rare disease that afflicts one child in the district without championing more common health concerns that do not have a face.

Such was the case for Steny Hoyer, a twelve-term Democrat from Mechanicsville, Maryland, who, as minority whip in the U.S. House of Representatives, is one of the most powerful members of Congress. To the Smith family who attend Representative Hoyer's church, that meant they got to share their story with a member of Congress. The Smiths' daughter,

Illustration 2.1. Five Conversations Your Legislators Want to Have

1. What the Local Statistics Are

Lawmakers have access to an extraordinary amount of information, but much of it is aggregate state or national data. Constituents can present insights directly from the district, a welcome and essential component of sound legislative decision-making.

2. How State or Federal Money is Being Spent in the District

State and federal legislators are interested in how government-run programs actually benefit their constituents, especially if it can be demonstrated that the funding provides tangible benefits and is responsibly managed.

3. Real-life Life Stories That Illuminate the Statistics

U.S. Capitols seem to be run by statistics, but these numbers remain meaningless until they can be understood in a real-life context. Personal stories help legislators understand your issues and make your position compelling. Stories are also easily used in floor speeches and news media sound bites.

4. Your Visibility and Connections Within the District

Local organizers, doctors, clergy, teachers, and business owners may all be "opinion leaders" in their respective communities. Legislators are aware that other voters may follow their lead.

5. The Specific Legislative Action That Would Make You Happy

Legislators never like to say no to constituents, but they must often choose between a multitude of actions that address any particular issue. Make your request specific.

Kristi, suffers from Rett's syndrome, a rare neurological disorder seen almost exclusively in girls. Kristi had lost communication skills and purposeful use of her hands. Through Kristi's father, Representative Hoyer learned about the illness and became passionately inspired by Kristi's story. He committed himself to educating Congress about the need to fund medical research related to Rett's syndrome and helped to amass $35 million in federal appropriations to study the disorder. Representative Hoyer was even able to get Hollywood on board when actress Julia Roberts agreed to testify on Rett's syndrome before the House Labor, Health and Human Services, and Education Appropriations Subcommittee about the disease. As a result of federally funded research, Dr. Huda Zoghbi discovered the gene related to Rett's syndrome. Treatment prospects now look hopeful. All this was in response to the plight of one little girl from Hoyer's district in Maryland.

Here's an example on the state level. In Maryland, because the news media were heavily focused on a legislative battle to allow slot machines in the state, public sentiment was well accounted for in the newspapers and on the television news. What Maryland Delegate Stanley Rosenberg sought as a central part of his individual decision-making process on the issue were the individual concerns related to slot machines that applied to the neighborhoods in the district he represents. Since these communities are in close proximity to a proposed slots location, he scheduled meetings in the district to solicit community viewpoints. He then asked his constituents to put their concerns down in writing to help him collect and manage the array of different viewpoints. Delegate Rosenberg did not seek letters that only said whether a constituent supported or opposed slot machines. He sought substantive insights as to what aspects of the proposed bill were most important to his voters. In other words, Delegate Rosenberg was very interested in listening to his constituents, especially if they provided thoughtful local information on the issue.

Do not worry if you do not have a professor's command of statistics or the lobbyist's range of arguments. You don't need them. You are a voter, a member of a family, someone who works in the district (or nearby), maybe even a community activist. This provides you with everything you need to lobby your elected officials effectively.

A brief letter illustrated with an interesting local story can wield tremendous power in a legislative office. It can neutralize a whole mailbag of preprinted postcards that your opposition has had its supporters merely sign and mail. Example 2.1 shows the differences between a formal argument and a personal story.

Example 2.1. Examples of the Difference Between Formal Argument and Personal Story

Example	Argument versus Personal Story
	Survivor: Lisa Bayha, Warwick, Rhode Island
	Issue: Stroke Research Funding

Formal Argument	Personal Story
Heart disease is America's no. 1 killer. Stroke is the nation's no. 3 cause of death. Despite the fact that heart disease, stroke, and other cardiovascular diseases are America's deadliest and costliest diseases, research to prevent, treat, and cure them is disproportionately underfunded.	I had my first stroke when I was twenty-one years old in May 1997, just one week before college graduation. You may be surprised to discover that someone so young could have a stroke. I was too. One moment I was a young woman reaching for a bright future, and the next I was a stroke patient.
	Luckily, I've regained almost all of my ability to move and talk, but I'm checked frequently by my physician. I'm still on many medications, some of which are old, some that are new, that I take regularly to prevent another stroke. I may be on these or other medications for the rest of my life. But I am in remission of the disease, so I'm on the way up.

My hope is that research will continue to improve the chances for survival for those who have strokes and improve the quality of life for those of us who make it, like me.

Example   Argument versus Personal Story:
Professional/Business Owner: Shelby Wilbourn, M.D.,
Belfast, Maine
Issue: Tort Reform

Formal Argument	Personal Story
Medical liability reform protects women's access to health care and provides ob-gyns with affordable and available medical liability insurance.	Last March I received a letter from my malpractice insurance carrier that my premiums were going to be increasing from $33,000 a year to approximately $108,000.
	This type of dramatic increase was impossible to deal with, so after twelve years, I closed my ob-gyn practice, leaving behind eight thousand patients and six loyal staff, some of whom had been with me since the very beginning. I relocated to another state where liability insurance premiums are a little more affordable and started all over again.
	I did not want to say goodbye to my staff, and I especially hated to see my patients go, but I just could not find a way to continue practicing medicine in our state with the ways things are now. The really sad part is that I am not the only doctor who has left. I am one of many doctors who have left.

(Continued)

Example 2.1. Continued

Example	Argument versus Personal Story
	Concerned Individual: Colleen Stack, Kansas City, Missouri
	Issue: Epilepsy Research Funding

Formal Argument	Personal Story
The Epilepsy Foundation urges Congress to support a major expansion of epilepsy research within the National Institutes of Health. These investments in our nation's health are paying dividends. In the past decade, considerable progress has been made in identifying genes associated with epilepsy and in developing medications, devices, and surgical treatments.	The reason for my involvement in advocacy for persons with epilepsy is my daughter who began having seizures at age ten. Increased funding is essential to finding a cure for epilepsy. Implantable devices may one day be able to abort pending seizures, gene research may lead to gene therapy, and new medications are being developed that provide new hope in a previously hopeless situation. The most important thing is that investment in research will improve the quality of life for your constituents like my daughter and their families. With your help, we can reach the goal of: no seizures, no side effects, and no stigma.

WHAT IF I DON'T HAVE AN EMOTIONALLY CHARGED PERSONAL STORY?

Ah, but you do. Remember that the fact that you are a voter, living in a legislator's district, means you cannot fail to be interesting and important to that elected official. If you do not have direct, personal experience with a given issue, don't let that dissuade you. Just remember to stress that you are sincerely concerned about an issue, though perhaps not personally affected by it. You are still a voter, or a contributor, or a volunteer, or a community leader, and the issues that matter to you will matter to your elected officials.

It should go without saying that you never want to lie—ever—in your communications with elected officials. In order to listen to you, your elected

Advice from the Field

Jane Weirich

Deputy Director of Nationwide Field Advocacy

American Cancer Society

"When we organized our national advocacy event called Celebration on the Hill, our strategy was to bring cancer survivors from every congressional district in the country, and we achieved that goal. Getting a constituent is a crucial part of getting a Congress member to pay attention, and we believed that there were great stories of cancer survival in every single congressional district in this country. We made it our challenge to find those stories and then scheduled our meetings on the Hill."

officials have to trust you. In terms of your personal story, never embellish or employ any literary license to make your story more dramatic or more "perfect." An elected official can usually smell a lie at ten paces.

REASONS TO BECOME POLITICALLY INVOLVED IN AN ISSUE

So what are your issues? Here are some of the reasons everyday citizens become drawn to advocacy:

- You or someone you love has experienced a life-changing event. Perhaps a loved one is diagnosed with a rare form of cancer and you want to do everything possible to support research.

- Someone personally asks you to join. Perhaps one of your friends is sent overseas as a member of the U.S. military, and for the first time, you ask for information about what you can do to help support the effort. Maybe you end up joining a grassroots network.

- You have been angered by something that the government has done. Perhaps one of those new traffic cameras photographs you going through a red light, and you are sent a ticket despite the fact that you were in a funeral procession. You decide that you will become involved in fighting this new technology.

- It occurs to you that the government should be doing more on a given issue. Perhaps you have discovered that builders want to put a development in a wooded area that you had believed was conservation land. When you discover that it is not protected, you decide to lead the charge to limit development.

- Through your work, studies, or other experience, you have become an expert on some issue that the government is grappling with. Perhaps you are a professor at a nearby university who has done research into the psychological aspects related to the recruitment of terrorists, and you have professional insights that you feel the need to share with your elected officials, even if they have not previously solicited your opinion.

- The work you do is affected by government regulation or reimbursement issues. Perhaps you are a doctor who sees patients who rely on Medicare. Treatment funding for these patients is provided in part by the federal government, and you realize that your ability to provide quality health care depends on what the government considers appropriate treatment and how much it pays for specific procedures.

- You discover that the opposition to an issue you care about, but have never taken action on, is well organized and vehement. Sometimes you have to learn the hard way that if you remain silent, the otherwise good intentions of our representatives will be swayed by the vocal.

- And a reason not to become politically active: Perhaps you are just plain mean and hopelessly inconsolable. Politics seems to attract people who are less interested in fighting for an issue than just having a place where they can vent.

YOUR PERSONAL ADVOCACY INVENTORY

Take a few moments to consider the questions in Worksheet 2.1 before you begin to communicate with your lawmakers on an issue. These questions should help steer you toward the kinds of district-based, individual information you already possess that can help support the issues you care about when you communicate with your elected officials.

Your Personal Advocacy Inventory

For each of the following questions, brevity is key. Allow yourself no more than one minute to verbally answer any one of these questions:

- What is your name? Where do you live? Where do you work? Describe your family.

  _____

- What originally sparked your interest in the issue you want to fight for?

  _____

- How has your life been changed, altered, or enriched by the issue?

  _____

- What is (or was) your occupation? (If you are in school, what do you hope your occupation will be?) Does your occupation give you any special insight into the issue?

  _____

- Do you know which level of government (federal, state, or local) would be most appropriate to address the issue?

  _____

- Do you have a specific request of your representative that is related to this issue?

  _____

- If your request were supported and made law, how do you think it would help address the issue—specifically in your life or the lives of your neighbors?

  _____

- Can you explain how any government funding currently related to the issue tangibly helps you or someone you know?

  _____

- In what ways are you active or visible in your community (in church, clubs, or civic organizations, for example)?

  _____

- Do you feel news media coverage of the issue has been accurate and informative? If not, what neglected aspects should your neighbors be made aware of?

  _____

- Are you a registered voter?

  _____

- Did you make any campaign contributions and did you volunteer for any local campaigns during the last election?

  _____

Identify Your Representatives

In this chapter, you will learn:

- Basic differences between your federal, state, and local governments
- Easy ways to identify your representatives at every level of government
- Basic contact, party, voting, and other information you want to record about each of your elected officials
- The importance of legislative staff to your advocacy efforts
- Why to take note of committee assignments related to your elected officials

Don't feel too bad if you have absolutely no idea who your elected representatives are. As much as political science professors like to decry our waning lack of political involvement, the fact is that blissful ignorance of the government, while perhaps not advisable, is nonetheless our birthright as Americans. In a totalitarian dictatorship, you need to know who is in charge because you need to watch your back (and besides, there are usually a lot of statues and pictures to constantly remind you that you are subjugated). In the United States, you can fail your civics class in high school and not be put in jail or asked to leave the country. You don't even have to vote in our country if you do not want to. There is a drawback, of course: the fewer Americans who feel any connection to, responsibility for, or interest in our government, the more our government, and all of its considerable power, gets abandoned to the relative few who do care, but perhaps not in the same way you do.

HOW IS OUR GOVERNMENT ORGANIZED?

Generally, most Americans have to deal with three levels of government: federal, state, and local (Illustration 3.1). It would be nice to say that each of these three levels of government is in charge of discrete issue areas and that if you were interested in education, for example, you simply needed to write to your state representatives. Homeland security? Your federal representative. Unfortunately, things are more complicated than that.

Let's start with the federal government. The federal government consists of three branches: executive, legislative, and judiciary. The federal government is usually characterized by the president of the United States. From a grassroots standpoint, it's good if the president feels passionately in favor of the issues you care about—but communicating your opinions directly to the president can be difficult, and with grassroots it's all about access. The president is necessarily surrounded by many protective security rings—but there are other rings around him besides, because the president of the United States has major staff. To get to him, you generally have to get by one of his formidable underlings, advisers, communications gatekeepers, cabinet members. It's usually hard to get him on the phone.

Sure, you can call or write the White House. The White House always attempts to seem open and accessible to the thoughts and feelings of all concerned Americans, but the sheer volume of correspondence takes a number of impersonal systems to manage. There is a staff of correspondents who handle the mail. Phone calls to the White House are put through a comments line, a sophisticated computer system that attempts to document your call without interrupting the latest peace summit to ask the president to pick up the phone.

32

Illustration 3.1. Levels of Government in the United States

State Government:
Issue areas: Some aspects of health care, education, driver licenses, voting and elections, state taxes, etc. Often bi-cameral, meaning there are two houses and you have elected representation in each.

○ **Local Government:**
Issue areas: Police, water, power, parking, etc.

Your city council district (local).

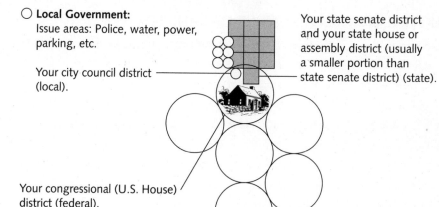

Your state senate district and your state house or assembly district (usually a smaller portion than state senate district) (state).

Your congressional (U.S. House) district (federal).

Federal Government:
Issue areas: Some aspects of health care, defense, monetary regulation, interstate commerce, federal taxes, etc. Each state has two senators in the U.S. Senate (both represent you) and one member in the U.S. House of Representatives.

Other realities impose themselves between you and access to the president. The president represents the entire country—every single one of us. When you write or call the president, you are but one of several hundred million people. And it doesn't end there. The president is the current title holder in the ongoing, always entertaining championship fight between the political parties, and often feels responsible, to some degree, to the current health and future prospects of his political party. And let's not forget that the president of the United States is arguably the most powerful leader in the world and is ultimately responsible for representing the United States in negotiations with every other country in the world.

There are other options for interacting with the federal government. That brings us to the legislative branch and Congress, where you have three elected officials who are far more accessible than the president and far more likely to respond to you.

Every state has two senators who represent its citizens in the U.S. Senate. Both senators represent the entire state (it is not divided between them). Then there is the House of Representatives. Every American (who does not live in the District of Columbia or another territory) has a representative in the U.S. House of Representatives. This lawmaker is responsible to and elected from a single congressional district and generally represents fewer than a million people.

In terms of grassroots communications, your U.S. senators and your representative in the House are far more accessible than the president. And here is the best part: they are more interested in what you have to say. Your senators and your House member know that no matter how many interest groups come into their offices to plead their case, no matter how many political action committees contribute to their reelection campaigns, you are one of those special people who can vote to keep them in office, and that right puts you in a powerful position. In general, your elected federal representatives want to make you happy if they can and avoid making you angry.

In addition to the federal government, you are also subject to state and local governments.

Your state government has as its executive a governor, who, like the president, manages a sizable portion of the state government, is the official voice of the state, and represents the spoils of the winning political party on the state level. Like the president, your governor may be difficult to contact directly, but nearly every state has a legislative branch very similar in organizational structure to the federal government. You might have to do a bit of research to uncover just how your state government is organized, but in general, most states have something similar to the federal Senate and House of Representatives. In California, for example, every resident has one state senator (as opposed to the two senators we each enjoy on the federal level) and one state assembly member (much like the representative in the U.S. House of Representatives). The state assembly member may be called a "delegate" or a state "representative," depending on the state. On the state level, the districts tend to be geographically smaller than on the federal level, but your state elected officials remain as accessible and genuinely interested in your communications.

The geographical boundaries of your congressional district (the area your representative in the U.S. House is responsible for) and your state legislative districts are often completely different. What remains the same is that the place where you sleep, eat, and pay bills is used to determine who represents you at every level of government.

There are other differences between the federal and state governments. Your state government may have term limits, meaning that any of your state representatives can hold office for only a predetermined period of time before he cannot run again for the same office. Your state legislature might convene only once a year for a brief period of time, in contrast to the U.S. Congress, which tends to be in session throughout the year.

Your local government might be organized like the federal government, with an executive and a legislative body, or it might be organized in a different way altogether. A typical way that local governments are organized includes a mayor in the executive function and a city council to perform the legislative function. On the local level, it is common to have a unicameral government, meaning one such body—a city council, for example. An elected mayor generally gets the media attention and gets to manage the majority of local government, but some local jurisdictions hire a city manager to fill this role and report to the city council.

The general principle employed by every level of government is that even if someone like a president, governor, or mayor is elected to be in charge, that person must work with and answer to a legislative body. Officially, this is called the sharing of powers and includes our judicial system, which, with its own set of unique powers, balances the actions of the executive and legislative branches. For instance, the judicial branch has the power to declare a law unconstitutional, even if the executive and legislative branches have achieved the extraordinarily difficult task of cooperating enough to pass a law.

As a grassroots advocate, you will focus on the legislative branch at every level of government for two reasons. The first has been explained: your legislative representatives are the best place for you to interact with your government. The second is that your federal, state, and local legislatures are where laws are introduced, amended, and sent to the executive to be signed into law. This is where the real action is on the issues you care about. More money for medical research? You have to convince the U.S. Congress to pass an appropriations bill. Implement a new program in your child's school? You might have to request a state representative to sponsor that bill in the state legislature. Tired of how long it takes your local utilities to repair downed power lines? Your city council must engage in oversight of their contracts.

There might also be an assortment of other government bodies whose actions affect you—things like school districts, water districts, and cemetery districts, with elected or appointed officials, all waiting for your input should you wish to become involved.

You do not need to master the various processes and organizational charts of every level of government where you live. Sometimes it is helpful, but that knowledge will come in time as you become more active as a constituent. What is required is that you know why you care about a specific issue—how it affects your family, loved ones, neighborhood, schools, work, or something else. Beyond that, you only need to get the mailing addresses of your elected officials to get started.

SO WHO REPRESENTS ME?

The Internet has greatly simplified the once laborious task of identifying federal, state, and local officials. There are a number of Web sites that can take your zip code (in some cases, your zip +4 is required—this information is also easily available on the Internet) and tell you the number of the federal, state, and local districts you live in and who currently represents those districts—and by extension, who represents you. The Internet Tips at the end of this chapter list Web sites that can help you with districting yourself at every level of government.

If you do not have Internet access, you can call your state registrar of voters and ask for your federal, state, and local district numbers and representatives. Alternatively, state political parties are usually happy to indulge questions about legislative districts. For ease of use, however, nothing beats the Internet, where you can easily discover who represents you and immediately get their contact information: office addresses, phone numbers, e-mail addresses, pictures, committee assignments, and more.

WHICH LEVEL OF GOVERNMENT HANDLES MY ISSUES?

Once you have accepted the fact that you are subject to federal, state, and local government, each with its own executive, legislative, and judicial components, you'd think it would be easy to determine which level of government handles which issue.

Sorry.

Let's start again at the top. There are some things that only the federal government can do. Declaring war, negotiating treaties, regulating foreign trade, printing money, and providing for the national defense are all policy areas reserved for the federal government.

Your state government has a few distinct issue areas as well. It regulates your elections, driver's licenses, and property taxes. Beyond that, assigning issue areas to specific levels of government quickly gets murky.

Your state government might traditionally be thought of as the arbiter of all education issues. However, the federal government might provide funding for specific programs that your state is ever so desperate to get its hands on—and that funding might come with some strings attached. So who is in charge of education: the federal government, state government, or local government? The answer is yes.

One of the pressures that muddies the playing field of issues between multiple levels of government is that elected officials have to run for office every so often. When they run for office, it helps if they can discuss the issues that voters care about, even if that level of government doesn't traditionally have jurisdiction over those issues. Your Congress members have no traditional authority over local police issues, but if they put their minds to it, they can find something that the federal government can do related to local public safety if that will get voters to the polls. Education, health care, and jobs are all huge issues that candidates at every level of government like to address on the campaign trail. Once in office, they might be limited in what they can deliver, but even small pieces of funding can have the effect of increasing the authority of one level of government in an issue area traditionally reserved for another level.

One-Hour Rule

Keep an up-to-date list of your representatives at every level of government and how to contact them. In that way, you are always ready to communicate with the people who have the authority and the incentive to act on your behalf.

The second pressure is money. The federal government has huge financial resources that state and local governments like to take advantage of, and money from the federal government always comes with strings attached. Say the federal government wanted to raise the legal smoking age across the country to twenty-one. States might balk at the federal government telling their citizens at what age they can smoke. However, the federal government could provide completely voluntary highway funding for states that have a smoking age of twenty-one. Suddenly, the states are listening and might be quite accommodating. Your federal representatives can then use the issue to run for reelection instead of relying on more abstract federal issues like interstate commerce.

THINGS YOU WANT TO KNOW ABOUT YOUR ELECTED OFFICIALS

There is some basic information that you need to know about your elected officials. When you fill out Worksheet 3.1, that information will be in one place.

You will notice that the worksheet asks you to record not only the name of your representatives, but the names and titles of any staff who work for them. Any sales executive will tell you that if you want to get through to important people, you need to befriend their staff. The same is true for advocates. It is helpful to jot down the names of receptionists and

Advice from the Field

John L. Jackley

Former Hill staffer and author of *Hill Rat* (1992)

"We frequently receive letters from all parts of the country on major issues. We throw these away. If you send these letters, I am sorry; the congressman gets reelected by 500,000 people. And you are not one of them."

From the book *Hill Rat: Blowing the Lid Off Congress* by John L. Jackley. Copyright © 1992 by Henry Regnery Publishing Inc. All rights reserved. Reprinted by special permission of Regnery Publishing Inc., Washington, D. C.

Critical Pieces of Information About Your Elected Officials

Keep one worksheet on each one of your elected officials.

1. Level of government (circle one):

   Federal   State   Local

2. Your district number:

   _____

3. Correct spelling of representative's full name:

   _____

4. Political party of representative:

   _____

5. Contact information

   Capitol office

   Address: _____

   Phone: _____

   Fax: _____

   E-mail: _____

   Local office

   Address: _____

   Phone: _____

   Fax: _____

   E-mail: _____

6. Committee assignments (do any of these committees handle the issues you care about?):

   _____

7. Staff names and titles:

Receptionist: _____

Phone: _____

E-mail: _____

Legislative assistant (who handles your issues): _____

Phone: _____

E-mail: _____

Scheduler (for scheduling in-person meetings): _____

Phone: _____

E-mail: _____

Legislative director: _____

Phone: _____

E-mail: _____

8. Known campaign contributors:

_____

9. Voting record on your issues:

_____

10. Characterize this legislator on your issues:

    Helpful   Indifferent   Unhelpful

11. What issues is this legislator primarily concerned with? Consider his or her voting record, press releases, and the legislator's background. Is there any overlap with the issues you are concerned about?

_____

12. Keep a record of the dates of your contacts with this office (including letters, phone calls, and in-person meetings, and the specific actions you requested).

_____

The One-Hour Activist by Christopher Kush. Copyright © 2004 Christopher Kush. To purchase this or other nonprofit titles from Jossey-Bass, please visit www.josseybass.com/go/nonprofit.

legislative assistants as you speak with them, and it is critical that you treat them professionally and with respect.

Keep this information up to date. Your elected officials do change, especially if your state has term limits, and a politician can stay in office only for a specific amount of time. Even if the incumbents stay, their staff changes. Office locations change, as do e-mail addresses, fax numbers, and phone numbers. Try to update your lists at least once every year.

WHY ARE COMMITTEE MEMBERSHIPS SO IMPORTANT?

The U.S. Congress considers some ten thousand bills every session (a session is two years). Any elected member of the U.S. House or Senate can introduce or sponsor legislation, and they do. The committee structure that our federal government and most state and local governments employ is, first and foremost, a way to divide up the work to get it done. Committees are generally divided up by issue area: health, armed services, education, and so forth. In Congress, there are not only full committees, but subcommittees established to be able to handle the avalanche of legislation that Congress members introduce every session.

The members of these committees can be extraordinarily powerful for a variety of reasons, and you always want to be aware if one of your representatives sits on a key committee that oversees the issues you care about. If your representative does not sit on such a committee, you are not allowed to simply adopt a more powerful member. But you can ask your representative to speak directly with a powerful committee chair as a way to help the district.

Once a bill is introduced, it is usually assigned to an appropriate committee for consideration. The members of that committee get to amend the bill and vote on it long before the bill arrives on the floor of the House or Senate. Committees also hold public hearings on bills, giving advocates on both sides of an issue the opportunity to address those members who have the most powerful voice on a particular bill.

Committee members often acquire a degree of expertise that other members of the U.S. House and Senate (or state legislature) generally defer

Internet Tip

Use the House and Senate Web sites to identify your members of Congress: House: http://www.house.gov/; Senate: http://www.senate.gov.

To find out your state and local representatives, try the Library of Congress State and Local Governments Internet Resource Page: http://www.loc.gov/global/state/stategov.html

To find federal voting records of your elected officials, try Project Vote Smart: http://www.vote-smart.org/.

Federal voting records are also available at THOMAS: http://thomas.loc.gov/.

State voting records may also be available through the office Web site of your state legislature: http://www.loc.gov/global/state/stategov.html.

To find who had made financial contributions to your elected officials, try any of the following,

> *Project Vote Smart: http://www.vote-smart.org/*
> *Federal Election Commission: http://www.fec.gov/*
> *Center for Responsive Politics: http://www.opensecrets.org/*

to. It is far less likely that a random member, who does not reside on the committee that handles an issue in question, will suggest extensive changes on the floor after those on the committee have considered, improved, and reported (passed) a specific piece of legislation out of committee.

All of these qualities conspire to make committee members extraordinarily powerful. If your elected officials reside on a committee related to the issues you care about, you are in luck: your representative can be more helpful than most others. It is more important than ever for you to share your stories or your expertise with your representative. If your member is not on a key committee, you still need to be active. A member who is not on a key committee still wields a floor vote, and sometimes the interest in a particular bill outside of a committee can exert pressure to make sure the bill is brought up for consideration and a vote instead of dying in committee from complete disinterest.

Join an Interest Group

Local institutions are to liberty what primary schools are to science; they put it within the people's reach; they teach people to appreciate its peaceful enjoyment and accustom them to make use of it.

—Alexis de Tocqueville, *Democracy in America*

In this chapter, you will learn:

- The difference between special interest groups and public interest groups
- How joining an interest group can make you a more informed and more efficient advocate
- Your Organized Interest Group Bill of Rights
- What Action Alerts are and how they can help make you a constituent to be reckoned with

As a rule, Americans loathe interest groups that they are not members of and generally laud, with warm declarations of patriotism, the groups that they are ideologically in concert with. Sometimes a distinction is made between "special" interest groups that fight for the narrow interests of their membership, like trade associations that focus on the needs of a specific profession (accountants or doctors, for example), and "public" interest groups that fight on behalf of good government for everyone's benefit, like environmental organizations that would argue that their work on behalf of the environment benefits all Americans. I refer to both types of groups collectively as "organized interest groups" or simply "interest groups" and make no moral distinction between them. These organizations exist, among other reasons, to help educate and influence the government in a given issue area. From a grassroots standpoint, special interest groups and public interest groups often employ the tools outlined in this book as part of their overall legislative strategy, which might include direct lobbying, campaign donations, and grassroots organizing.

The lobbying that interest groups engage in is not all about lunch—even if the lunches tend to be very nice ones. Organized interest groups often hire lobbyists who must identify, analyze, and monitor the thousands of individual bills introduced in any particular session of Congress or the state legislature that might have an impact on the membership of their group. At the same time, they often work on crafting their own legislation and getting elected officials to sponsor it. As experts, they are sometimes called on to testify in front of government bodies. Organized interest groups are usually the first interview stop for news media covering a story that deals with their issues. If there is a political action committee (PAC) component to the organization, interest group staff might be busy identifying and supporting or opposing candidates for office. And finally, the staff of organized interest groups are inevitably frustrated and bored to death by the dozens of meetings they usually have to attend in any given week, all the while maintaining a confident and committed stance in the face of relentless attacks from the opposition.

BENEFITS OF JOINING WITH OTHERS

Of course, you are free to remain a lone wolf in the political process. You can choose to avoid organized interest groups altogether and personally engage in as many of the aforementioned time-consuming and often thankless tasks as you would like to, but why re-invent the wheel? For a reasonable membership fee, organized interest groups will worry about identifying key bills related to the issues you care about and identify opportunities for grassroots input for you. They might even invite you to come to the state capitol and set up face-to-face meetings with your elected officials.

All things considered, joining an organized interest group is a great way for you to advance the issues that you believe in and manage your grassroots participation without having to give up other important aspects of your life.

Joining an organized interest group also helps you act in concert with other like-minded advocates. Through active, articulate grassroots networks, organized interest groups can coordinate the letters, calls, and meetings needed to secure support in a large number of legislative offices (remember the Grassroots Drive-In). If they do their work correctly, an interest group can ensure that your letters have the maximum chance of advancing the issues you care about.

One-Hour Rule

Before you join an organized interest group, make sure it offers an effective grassroots network.

But be careful. Not all organized interest groups have viable grassroots networks, and you want to be judicious about giving money to a group that has no vision for how *you* can actively help fight for the issues you care about. You might also be wary of interest groups that relegate their grassroots networks to low-impact communications like preprinted postcards and prewritten e-mail messages.

YOUR ORGANIZED INTEREST GROUP BILL OF RIGHTS

Here are some of the advocacy-related benefits that sophisticated interest groups should provide as part of their membership benefits.

Background on the Issue

An organized interest group must constantly educate lawmakers and the news media about an issue, so they should have plenty of excellent background materials to help educate you about an issue you may care about but not completely understand in terms of related legislative battles.

Legislative Agenda

An interest group should have a list of current bills that it is monitoring, opposing, supporting, or attempting to amend. This helps focus your attention on the federal, state, and local bills related to the issues you care about. (See Action 5 for more on legislative agendas.)

Grassroots Mobilization

You should be notified when your grassroots input is helpful, either through an Action Alert or personally by the organization's staff. When your group asks you to weigh in on a piece of legislation, it should supply you with a summary of the bill in question, an explanation of where it is in the process, a clearly stated request that will help you stay on message with the rest of their grassroots network, and maybe even a sample letter or phone script that you can customize with your own personal story.

Voting Records

At the end of the day (or the session), the only thing that matters is how your elected officials voted on the issues that matter to you. Their vote is binding. Your organized interest group should create a voting report card or similar device to help you keep track of how your representatives voted on the issues you care about.

Access to Staff

If you need more information or would like to be more actively involved with the decision-making process of an interest group, the staff of the organization should be friendly, attentive, and helpful. Be wary of any special interest group that is so busy rushing around that its staffers habitually ignore the requests and input of their membership. There is no shortage of organized interest groups that waste time and money without accomplishing any discernable victories. You do not need to waste your money on a well-meaning effort that leads to naught.

Local News Media Connections

Just as an organized interest group should inform you when your input is needed in Washington, D.C., or your state capitol, an effective organized interest group will also make use of its membership for news media relations by fielding actual members for interview requests from local news media. Again, any organized interest group that does not provide news media training or otherwise trust you in this regard probably does not understand how to use the news media effectively to generate awareness about your issue.

Staying on Message

Sometimes people who cannot stand to take direction join organized interest groups and then are surprised that interest group organizers request that everyone who participates in their Action Alerts stay on message, almost as if democracy itself was being stolen from them. You have a responsibility as a member of an organized interest group that prevents you from discussing unrelated issues or other side issues when you are responding to an Action Alert. These organizations are not the guardians of your democracy. If you disagree with their positions or you have an interest outside their purview, you can and should simply choose not to participate in their Action Alerts.

WHAT IS AN ACTION ALERT?

One of the real advantages of becoming a member of an interest group is that it can mobilize you when your input can exert the maximum impact on the issue in question. Interest groups often send out an Action Alert to do this. An Action Alert is a brief one- to two-page notice that urges you (and others) to take immediate action on a specific bill, usually by writing to or calling your elected officials. Action Alerts are generally distributed by e-mail, but they can come by fax, in the mail, even by phone.

Most Action Alerts provide a brief description of the issue in question, an explanation of why now is the time to act, and a sample letter or phone script to make participation easy. Just remember to personalize any sample communication provided on the Action Alert to make your letter and phone call an individual piece of communication (but state the actual request verbatim so that you stay on message).

A typical Action Alert has these parts:

- Date and headline. This helps to identify the message as timely and should grab your attention by telling what is at stake.

Advice from the Field
Michael Crawford
Associate Field Director
Human Rights Campaign

"When people join with others through an organization, the power of the individual is magnified. Advocacy groups can help to focus the energy and passion of many individuals in a single direction that will maximize the chances of accomplishing our common political goals."

- Deadline and contact information. If several pieces of contact information are provided in an Action Alert, choose the method of communicating that is most convenient for you. The deadline should underscore that there is a window of opportunity for your input and for your voice to be heard.

- Message or request, including bill number and action. You should be asked to clearly state your request by bill number and desired action, for example, "Vote no on AB 342."

- Process update. The interest group should inform you of where in the process a particular bill is, and why it is imperative to correspond with legislators at this juncture. This not only helps letters be accurate, but it also makes you a more sophisticated advocate by educating you about the legislative process.

- Talking points. Succinct arguments that support the desired position and address opposition arguments should be included as part of the Action Alert. Some alerts provide a sample letter that can be used to help you get started with your own personalized letter. Avoid copying any sample letter verbatim. If you can write an original letter, you stand a far greater chance of convincing your lawmakers that you are informed and serious.

Create a Legislative Agenda

In this chapter, you will learn:

- How a bill becomes a law in the United States
- How a legislative agenda can help you keep track of how your federal, state, and local governments are addressing the issues you care about
- How to create a personal legislative agenda
- Four basic positions you can take on any bill
- Ten things you can ask your elected officials to do to help fight for the issues you care about

There are likely to be several bills that address the issues you care about during any given session of Congress or session of your state legislature. (Illustration 5.1 sets out how a bill becomes a law.) For example, a bill search in the current Congress identified fifty-two bills that have *abortion* as a key word. There are bills to prohibit so-called partial birth abortion, a proposed amendment to the Constitution making abortion illegal, proposed restrictions on the so-called abortion drug RU486, a bill to provide parental notification and intervention in the case of a teen seeking abortion. The list goes on and on, and this is just at the federal level. While fifty-two may seem a large number of bills, when you consider the fact that over ten thousand bills get introduced in every two-year session of Congress, you begin to see that if you cared about abortion-related issues, narrowing down

Illustration 5.1. How a Bill Becomes a Law

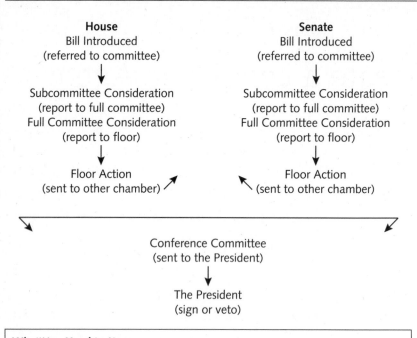

What You Need to Know:
- Every piece of legislation must survive numerous votes before final passage.
- Committee members play a more powerful role in the fate of your legislation than noncommittee members.
- Many tactics exist to expedite, stall, or circumvent this process.

the ten thousand introduced pieces of legislation to fifty-two that deal specifically with your issue might be helpful indeed.

Identifying the few bills you care about is critical to your effectiveness as an activist and usually involves making and managing what is called a legislative agenda.

WHAT IS A PERSONAL LEGISLATIVE AGENDA?

A personal legislative agenda is a listing of all of the bills that are related to the issues you care about—those you are supporting, those you are opposing, those you are just keeping an eye on, and those you want to see introduced.

At a glance, a legislative agenda helps you manage several key pieces of information related to the bills you are fighting for at a specific level of government and during a specific session. Items that are usually included in a legislative agenda are listed below:

• A list of current bills that relate to the issues you care about. This might be relegated to one specific level of government (bills in Congress, for example), but it should be exhaustive. You do not only want to list the bills that your interest group has introduced; you want to keep track of all the bills your opposition has introduced as well.

One-Hour Rule

Thousands of bills are introduced at every level of government every year. You will have the time and interest to follow only a few of them. A legislative agenda helps you to identify and focus on the few bills you care about.

• Your position on current bills. These are bills that have been formally introduced in the legislature:

Support—you want the bill to become law as written.
Oppose—you do not want the bill to become law as written.
Amend—you would support the bill if some changes were made to the legislation as it is currently written.
Watch—you might be interested in a bill but have no personal time to support or oppose it, or it may be that the bill would be dangerous but is so unpopular that it does not immediately require your advocacy efforts that can be more helpfully applied elsewhere.

• Your strategy or planned action for each bill. An interest group might have a complex strategy related to passing a piece of legislation that might include statewide or nationwide grassroots, the news media, and campaign donations. Remember that you are in charge of your elected officials and your elected officials only, so your strategy can be relatively simple: Will you write, call, or visit your representatives? Your strategy should also provide a sense of the amount of time you have to devote to these issues. Another common strategy would be to focus your attention on the bills where your representatives have the most power—for example, any that pass through key committees that your members sit on.

• Where the bill is currently located in the legislative process. Your legislative agenda helps you see at a glance where all the bills you care about are—whether they were just introduced, are being considered in committee, or are scheduled for a floor vote. Such information can help you determine the best time to speak up. If your representative sits on the committee that one of the bills on your legislative agenda must pass through, be sure to communicate with that person because he or she is especially powerful on that issue.

Advice from the Field

Justin Moore

Association Director, Federal Legislative Affairs

American Physical Therapy Association

"Providing a solid foundation of basic legislative information is crucial to getting our members involved and responsive to Action Alerts, calls, faxes, and e-mails. Another fundamental component is the updates we are able to provide on the issues we are following. Our members want to know they made a difference or if further action is needed. Our legislative agenda guides us through this communication."

• Updates and amendments. Updates help you revise your strategy as needed and keep track of any amendments or other changes that have been introduced by other groups. Your updates might also include political information, such as growing or dwindling support for the bill as reflected in polls from increased news media attention. Sometimes an update will lead you to rethink and revise your own position on a bill.

Use Worksheet 5.1 to organize your personal legislative agenda.

THINGS YOU CAN ASK A LAWMAKER TO DO TO HELP FIGHT FOR THE ISSUES YOU CARE ABOUT

Here is a list of ten common requests that activists make of lawmakers:

- Introduce legislation.
- Cosponsor legislation that has already been introduced.
- Vote for a specific piece of legislation.
- Vote against a specific piece of legislation.
- Introduce, support, or oppose an amendment to a specific piece of legislation.
- Make a speech on the floor of the House or Senate.
- Talk to another legislator who shares the same geography, party, committee assignment, or voting demographics.
- Talk to local news media about the issues or bills you care about.
- Visit your local organization or group to get a deeper understanding of your issues and to demonstrate support for your issues.
- Circulate or sign a "Dear Colleague" letter—not legislation but a letter that expresses support for an particular piece of legislation.

Remember that if you are taking action as part of an interest group or Action Alert, you must make the exact request that the rest of the group is making, or you risk going off message.

Worksheet: Personal Legislative Agenda

Personal Legislative Agenda

Level of Government: U.S. Senate

Date: 05/15

Bill number: S1234 (sample bill)

My position:

support   oppose   amend   watch

Description:

This bill would reauthorize the Individuals with Disabilities Education Act (I.D.E.A.) so that it could continue to receive funding for the next five years.

Process and updates:

(Where is the bill in the process? How has the bill been amended?)
The bill is currently in the Senate Health Committee. Hearings are planned for next month. Easter Seals has sent information that this bill could potentially incorporate several specific improvements over the current program.

My action:

 I sent a personal letter to both Senator Jones and Senator Smith explaining how I.D.E.A. has helped our Katie attend Prarie Elementary here in Montgomery. I mentioned the list of improvements supported by Easter Seals. (Senator Jones sent a letter back expressing her support. I am still waiting to hear from Senator Smith.)

Fate of this bill: Pending.

Bill number:

    My position:

    support   oppose   amend   watch

Description:

Process and updates:
(Where is the bill in the process? How has the bill been amended?)

My action:

Fate of this bill:

Bill number:

    My position:

    support   oppose   amend   watch

Description:

Process and updates:
(Where is the bill in the process? How has the bill been amended?)

My action:

Fate of this bill:

Analyze a Bill

In this chapter, you will learn:

- The parts of a federal bill
- Where to find a plain-English summary of proposed legislation
- How bill analysis can help you identify the bills that really need your support and those that do not
- Common justifications for increases in appropriations for programs you support

Lawmakers, government bodies, and organized interest groups all perform bill analysis: they try to anticipate, as accurately as possible, the effect a piece of legislation would likely have if signed into law. It is a critical part of their work. You, as an advocate, should not feel the need to duplicate their efforts by performing detailed legal or fiscal analysis of any pending legislation. Nevertheless, the Internet has made it possible for everyday Americans to download and review the actual text of legislation and there are several interesting things that advocates can glean from surveying pieces of pending legislation. For example, you can determine before a vote is taken whether your lawmaker has officially expressed support for the bill by becoming a cosponsor. You can read a plain-English summary of a bill for yourself to see what it hopes to accomplish and how it hopes to accomplish it.

The job of legislative staff and lobbyists is to assess the impact—political, economic, and social—of as many facets of a proposed piece of legislation as possible so that lawmakers can cast educated votes. Every piece of legislation sounds as if it would do something really great if enacted, but in reality, a significant law is difficult to craft and implement. Many lawmakers use bill analysis to avoid unintended consequences from legislation, which are always likely even in a good bill. Such unintended consequences might include an incredibly expensive program that does not provide tangible benefits for constituents.

When lobbyists, the White House, and the Congressional Budget Office engage in bill analysis, they are going to be far more specific than you need to be; they might use complex financial projections or make references to published research papers. It is not necessary for you to engage in such detail or to agonize over confidence intervals or other statistical analysis. Your bill analysis is not going to be submitted for publication, and your lawmakers and interest groups conduct their own analysis. Your bill analysis is for your own personal enlightenment: it is to help you understand and intelligently correspond on a bill.

Bills are written to conform with the existing code of law and often take the format of "legalese" (see Example 6.1). There may be numerous references in a bill to existing law in the form of code numbers and section numbers that generally do not mean anything to the layperson. Don't fret; bill language often is confounding to lawmakers themselves. For that reason, Congress and your state legislature often provide plain-English summaries of any proposed piece of legislation. Congress prepares what is called a *bill digest* version of major bills that you do not need a law degree to read and understand.

A good place to start with your bill analysis is to locate the text of a proposed piece of legislation on the Internet (alternatively, your representatives should be able to send you copies of any bills upon request; simply call the office). THOMAS, the Library of Congress's Web site, and probably your state's official Web site, provide on-line search engines that allow you to comb through current bills by subject area. Here again the advantage of joining an

Example 6.1. Example of a Federal Bill

Congress/ ———————— 108TH CONGRESS **S. RES. 108** ———————— Bill Number
Session   1ST SESSION

Title ———————————— Designating the week of April 21 through April 27, 2003, as "National
(more descriptive   Cowboy Poetry Week".
than bill number)

         ————————————   Chamber
                           (House/
         IN THE SENATE OF THE UNITED STATES ——————— Senate)

Date of ——————————————————————— APRIL 8, 2003
introduction
        Mr. BURNS (for himself, Mr. BAUCUS, Mr. BROWNBACK, Mr. HATCH, and Mr.
        REID) submitted the following resolution; which was referred to the Com- ——— Sponsor/
        mittee on the Judiciary   Committee
                                           referral

Bill type ———————————— **RESOLUTION**

        Designating the week of April 21 through April 27, 2003,
                as "National Cowboy Poetry Week".

        Whereas throughout American history, cowboy poets have
            played a large part in framing the landscape of the
            American West through written and oral poetry;

        Whereas the endurance of these tales and poems dem- ——— Bill text
            onstrates that cowboy poetry is still a living art;

        Whereas recognizing the contributions of these poets dates as
            far back as cowboys themselves; and

        Whereas it is necessary to recognize the importance of cow-
            boy poetry for future generations: Now therefore be it

     1   *Resolved,* That the Senate—

                        2 ——————————————— Bill page
                                              number

     1   (1) designates that week of April 21 through
     2   April 27, 2003, as "National Cowboy Poetry Week";
     3   and
     4   (2) requests the President to issue a proclama-
     5   tion calling upon the people of the United States to
     6   celebrate the week with the appropriate ceremonies,
     7   activities, and programs.

                              ○

(Continued)

Example 6.1. Continued

NEW SEARCH | HOME | HELP

S.RES.108
Title: A resolution designating the week of April 21 through April 27, 2003, as "National Cowboy Poetry Week".
Sponsor: Sen Burns, Conrad R. [MT] (introduced 4/8/2003)   **Cosponsors:** 4
Latest Major Action: 4/11/2003 Passed/agreed to in Senate. Status: Resolution agreed to in Senate without amendment and with a preamble by Unanimous Consent. b

Jump to: Titles, Status, Committees, Related Bill Details, Amendments, Cosponsors, Summary

TITLE(S): (*italics indicate a title for a portion of a bill*)

- OFFICIAL TITLE AS INTRODUCED:
  A resolution designating the week of April 21 through April 27, 2003, as "National Cowboy Poetry Week".

STATUS: (*color indicates Senate actions*) ——————————————— Status (Summarizes committee referrals and votes thus far)

4/8/2003:
  Referred to the Committee on the Judiciary. (text of measure as introduced: CR S4974)
  4/11/2003:
    Committee on the Judiciary. Ordered to be reported without amendment favorably.
4/11/2003:
  Committee on the Judiciary. Reported by Senator Hatch without amendment and with a preamble. Without written report.
4/11/2003:
  Placed on Senate Legislative Calendar under General Orders. Calendar No. 74.
4/11/2003:
  Resolution agreed to in Senate without amendment and with a preamble by Unanimous Consent. (consideration: CR S5393-5394; text as passed Senate: CR S5394)

COMMITTEE(S):

Committee/Subcommittee:	Activity:
Senate Judiciary	Referral, Markup, Reporting

RELATED BILL DETAILS:

NONE

AMENDMENT(S): ————————————————————— Amendments (changes made to original bill)

NONE

COSPONSORS(4), ALPHABETICAL [followed by Cosponsors withdrawn]:   (Sort: by date) ———— Sponsors (ardent supporters/ certain "yes" votes)

Sen Baucus, Max - 4/8/2003 [MT]   Sen Brownback, Sam - 4/8/2003 [KS]
Sen Hatch, Orrin G. - 4/8/2003 [UT] Sen Reid, Harry M. - 4/8/2003 [NV]

SUMMARY AS OF:
4/11/2003--Passed Senate, without amendment.   (There are 2 other summaries)

(This measure has not been amended since being introduced in the Senate on April 8, 2003. The summary of that version is repeated here.)

Designates the week of April 21 through 27, 2003, as National Cowboy Poetry Week.

Summary (provides a plain-English explanation of complex legislation) interest group shows itself: the interest group will usually provide bill numbers as part of their legislative agendas or Action Alerts. You can then use an on-line search engine to go directly to the bill you are interested in.

Print out the text of the bill along with any additional information (for example, about cosponsors or committee referrals) that is available. THOMAS provides a "Bill Summary and Status" page on each federal bill, and it is on this page that you will find the plain-English summary of the bill in question. This version should tell you what the bill hopes to accomplish, how it hopes to accomplish that goal, who will be in charge of implementing the new law, and where the money will come from to pay for it. In a nod toward fiscal responsibility, federal and state governments might include an estimate of how much this new law will likely cost to implement and to run over time. Finally, remember that legislation is often amended as it wends its way through the legislature, so continue to pay careful attention to the newspapers, your association updates, and maybe the Internet, to keep abreast of any changes that may have been made to your bill.

ADVANTAGES AND INSIGHTS PROVIDED BY BILL ANALYSIS

More than understanding what legislation actually proposes, good bill analysis can provide you and/or your organized interest group with a number of strategic insights:

• Bill analysis helps you identify bills that are helpful or potentially harmful. With the avalanche of legislation that is introduced at the federal and state levels of government every year, it is important to be able to identify the few bills worthy of your attention—those that can really make a difference and those that might really do some damage.

• Bill analysis helps you anticipate the potential consequences of a specific bill. A common trick of legislators is to give bills a nickname that makes them sound innocuous or inviting—the "Better Medicare Act" or the "Let's Make Our Schools Stronger Act." These titles, however, are more about window dressing than accurately characterizing the risks, costs, and liabilities related to a proposed piece of legislation. It is only by taking a close look at the details of a bill that you can determine if it is likely to help your cause or harm it, or if it is unlikely to make much of a difference.

• Bill analysis can help you identify potential coalitions. You might be able to identify other groups that will share your position on a bill and be able to boost a bill's attractiveness by demonstrating broad support for the bill from a variety of different constituencies.

• Bill analysis gives you a sense of timing. Part of your analysis can focus on the speed with which a specific piece of legislation is being considered and if there is still a window of opportunity for you to act on it. If you miss a key vote, your efforts might be rendered moot.

• You might be perfectly aware who your usual opponents will be, but bill analysis can sometimes help you anticipate those unexpected groups that might emerge in opposition to your legislation. (See Action 7.)

• Bill analysis gives you a handle on hyperbole. You can be an educated consumer of your own interest group's hype, so you are not easily manipulated by anyone—even those who are also fighting for the issues you care about.

• Bill analysis can help you identify the bills that will "move" and those that are "dead." Some of the most outrageous or potentially harmful pieces of legislation have the least chance for passage. The same can be said, at times, for good legislation that runs up against the contrary wishes of a powerful legislator. Bill analysis helps you to identify bills that need your help and those that won't be harmed or helped by your efforts either way—a powerful tool to help manage your time.

The bill analysis worksheet in Worksheet 6.1 will guide you in gathering the information you need.

One-Hour Rule

Never use your bill analysis as a way to develop lengthy formal arguments related to a piece of legislation or to replace your personal stories and expertise when talking about issues. If you do, you will be abandoning your greatest source of influence.

Bill Analysis Worksheet

Basic Information and Tracking

What level of government are you working with?

What is the bill number?

What is the title of the bill?

Are there any key words, phrases, or concepts associated with the bill?

Where does the bill currently reside (which committee)?

Is the bill scheduled for any upcoming hearings or votes?

Policy

What is the intent of the bill? (What problem does it hope to address, and what are its goals?)

What are the core provisions of the bill?

What are the estimated costs associated with the bill?

Do you think you can support this bill?

(Continued)

What are the three strongest reasons you have to support or oppose the bill?

1. _____

2. _____

3. _____

Politics

Is there any group or any legislators that oppose your position? Who are they?

1. _____

2. _____

3. _____

What are their most sound reasons for opposing your position?

1. _____

2. _____

3. _____

Does the bill have the support of the Leadership in the legislature?

_____

Do your representatives share your position on the issue?

_____

Have you educated them about your position?

_____

Do they sit on a committee that will deal with the legislation?

_____

Is there any way for you to use grassroots advocacy to support their position or pressure them to change their position?

_____

What would your message be?

_____

What is the deadline for such action?

_____

Did you write, call, or send a letter?

_____

Did you send a copy of your communications to your grassroots network or interest group?

_____

Did you receive a reply from your legislative office?

_____

How did your representative respond?

_____

What will the next formal action on this bill be (committee hearing, floor vote, etc.)?

_____

What day will that action take place?

_____

Do you know how your legislator voted on the bill?

_____

The One-Hour Activist by Christopher Kush. Copyright © 2004 Christopher Kush.
To purchase this or other nonprofit titles from Jossey-Bass, please visit
www.josseybass.com/go/nonprofit.

SHOW ME THE MONEY

Government-run programs generally have to be funded anew every year no matter how popular or how effective they are. Advocates are often put in the position of justifying funding for existing programs rather than constantly advocating for new and different programs to address the issues they care about. Lawmakers often share taxpayer skepticism about government-funded programs that constantly request increases without visible benefits to constituents.

Funding increases for existing programs must always be justified. Lobbyists justify funding increases by relying on statistics, but it is usually more effective for an activist if you can convince your representative that the pro-

Advice from the Field

Grayson Fowler

Manager, Federal Relations

Campaign for Tobacco-Free Kids

"Your time is better spent looking for a public interest group whose bill analysis you trust than doing your own. A public interest group not only can provide you with an analysis of legislation but also with detailed answers to any questions you have and an ongoing update of legislative actions. It's like having a small army of employees. But if you insist on going it alone and you're headed into committee action on a bill, try to get a copy of the "chairman's mark"—the version of the bill that the committee will actually consider, which may include a number of last-minute, and very significant, changes."

gram has tangible benefits to folks at home. You do not need to carry out extensive economic analysis here. It is most helpful to explain the human value of the program, but then be able to build on your personal stories with a substantive explanation of need. Here is a list of common justifications for increases in appropriations:

- There was a cut in funding from the previous fiscal year.

- There is a documented increase in need.

- The funding has never adequately met the need.

- The funding has been well spent, e.g., has low overhead and modest salaries.

- The program provides a tangible, cherished service to constituents.

- The program is innovative and has demonstrated effectiveness.

- Some of the program funding comes to the district.

- The program gets significant news media attention.

- The program saves the government money (for example, by avoiding more costly problems).

Internet Tip

To download federal legislation, use THOMAS: http://thomas.loc.gov.

To get information about how the federal budget affects your issues, try OMB Watch: http://www.ombwatch.org.

To find state and local legislative information, try Library of Congress State and Local Governments Internet Resource Page: http://www.loc.gov/global/state/stategov.html.

Conduct Opposition Research

In this chapter, you will learn:

- Simple ways to conduct opposition research
- How to approach opposition research without sacrificing your integrity
- How to distinguish among four kinds of opposition
- Compelling ways to counter the opposition's arguments with elected officials, the public, and the news media

A s much can be learned about a given issue from a study of the opposition as from its ardent supporters. Grassroots advocacy can make good use of such analysis. The opposition will gladly reveal the strongest arguments against your position. In fact, they will insist on trumpeting those arguments. This is extremely useful information, but only if you are able to listen without feeling threatened. The stronger their arguments are, the more important it is for you to understand them.

Too often, especially in campaigns for public office, opposition research is used to exploit humiliating personal details about another candidate and his or her family. Running for public office does involve some level of personal scrutiny, but it should not become so punishing an experience, so risky and exploitative, that we deter everyday citizens who could make a difference in office from ever running.

In that spirit, you can apply opposition research to your legislative priorities as a way to help you understand and prepare for the widest possible spectrum of constituencies affected by the policies you are promoting. You can do this without engaging in opposition research to personally destroy others who feel differently about an issue than you do.

Begin by acknowledging that opposition exists. There is not a policy issue in existence that does not harbor opposition on some level. *Everything has opposition.* Your first challenge is not to take the fact that opposition exists as a personal attack. Next, focus your opposition on the issues and the issues only—not the people who oppose you—no matter how tempting it might be to poke fun at the more extreme leaders of your opposition, even if you know something about them that they prefer not to have revealed.

To effectively counter their opposition, you must first genuinely understand them. Be careful here. Emotions can distort the arguments of your opposition in your ears and add all sorts of fantastic adornment in your head if you do not scrupulously dedicate yourself to understanding their arguments as they are actually intended.

It may be tempting, for example, to exaggerate your opposition's arguments as an easy way to refute them. There is no shortage of examples from special interest groups and political pundits who create outrageous speculations as to the consequences of a proposed bill or candidate. These efforts attempt to scare people into supporting your position or to make an issue seem so polarized that you can deny that there are any legitimate concerns on the other side. This is dishonest, it is lazy from an intellectual standpoint, and manipulating people in such a fashion ultimately degrades the quality of our public discourse. Don't do it.

If you are able to dispassionately identify where your opposition is coming from, your best bet for neutralizing the opposition is to acknowledge it and then to refute their positions with either pure logic or a personal appeal. Ignoring their arguments, dismissing them as silly, or refusing to talk about them does little to diminish your opposition's arguments. Any argument that is simply disregarded or radically distorted by the other side tends to remain intact. In the same way, personal attacks on your opposition do little to dismantle the intellectual or emotional appeal of the arguments they present.

Conducting opposition research can be as cursory or as time-consuming as you desire. The opposition is likely to engage in the similar grassroots actions that you use to bolster their position. That means you should easily find the opposition quoted in the newspaper, attending public hearings, writing letters to the editor, responding to Action Alerts, forming interest groups, getting out the vote on Election Day, and putting up Web sites that are full of strategic information for their supporters . . . and you. In fact, wherever you find the opposition, you are likely to find an abundance of helpful information. You will want to carefully process it rather than let it bother you.

In some cases, your opposition research will always be focused on marginalizing your opponents and discrediting their arguments. But such issues are relatively few when you consider the full spectrum of legislation introduced in any given year. Solid opposition research can often help you identify areas of compromise where there is a chance to neutralize the opposition by addressing their concerns—and thereby clear the way for passage of a bill you support.

A recent example is the provision of a prescription drug benefit for Medicare recipients. Many conservative Republicans in Congress abhorred establishing what they saw as an expensive new entitlement program. Their support was able to be secured, in part, by incorporating a new program conservatives cherished but had not been able to enact: the establishment of health care savings accounts that Americans could use to offset health care costs.

A final point to keep in mind about the opposition is that politics makes strange bedfellows. The deeper you delve into the American policy process, the more complex and nuanced the issues become. Your concerns about an issue may lead you to support or oppose many different and diverse pieces of legislation over time. Groups that constitute your opposition today may be your friends tomorrow. In fact, they might be friends on a different pending bill right now. This is all the more reason to keep your opposition activities focused on a specific piece of legislation. Operating with integrity will help you oppose your opposition on one piece of legislation and then join with them (with a minimal amount of poisoned feelings) on another.

EASY WAYS TO CONDUCT OPPOSITION RESEARCH

Opposition research can be surprisingly easy:

• Clipping articles, editorials, and interviews from the local newspaper will help you identify the individuals and organizations that oppose your issue. Note the stories and statistics they use to support their positions as well as their arguments. Judge for yourself how persuasive you feel their statements are, and use Worksheet 7.1 to counter any appealing arguments they present. (See Action 14 for how to start a press clippings file.)

• Join your opposition's grassroots networks. Your opposition's desire to mobilize large numbers of people often dictates that the gateways for joining their Action Alert mailing lists be minimally patrolled. Don't lie if questioned about the nature of your interest but consider providing your e-mail address or mailing address to an opposing interest group if it will provide access to their publications and Action Alerts. To be sure, you will be adding one more supposed supporter to the numbers they cite as grassroots support of their agenda, but the information you get as a result might be worth it.

• Search on-line. Your opposition probably has an on-line presence that highlights their legislative agenda and methodically articulates their strongest

One-Hour Rule
Focus on the policy, not the people. Any assertion that your opposition makes that is not first acknowledged and then respectfully countered will be assumed by lawmakers to be valid.

Preparing for the Opposition

Argument	Analysis	Counter-argument
Acknowledge the Arguments	Analyze the Arguments	Confront the Arguments
State each of your opposition's arguments in the strongest possible form. Do not editorialize.	• Does their argument play to emotion? • Does their argument rely on statistics? • Are they interpreting their statistics correctly? • Is their statement partially false or totally false? • Is their solution viable? • Are they accurately characterizing the problem? • Is your opposition a friend or an enemy?	Think of three possible responses for each argument.
Example: Some local bars and restaurants oppose the "clean indoor air" bill because they say a significant number of their customers will disappear if they are no longer allowed to smoke in their establishments.	This argument switches the focus from public health to the local economy. There is some emotional appeal in this argument. The image of disappearing customers would be frightening to any business owner. This argument is not backed up by any local polls. It is conjecture on the part of several local business owners.	1. I am a local customer. I frequently dine out, and the clean indoor air bill will encourage me to eat out more often. 2. The Campaign for Tobacco-Free Kids has documented that "smoke-free restaurant and bar laws do no harm to business." This is the result of a real study, not mere conjecture. 3. Local business owners should be aware that many complaints about second-hand smoke in bars and restaurants come from employees who may experience increased health risks—which translates into higher health-care premiums, lost productivity, and even lawsuits.

The One-Hour Activist by Christopher Kush. Copyright © 2004 Christopher Kush. To purchase this or other nonprofit titles from Jossey-Bass, please visit www.josseybass.com/go/nonprofit.

Advice from the Field

W. Minor Carter

Lawyer/Lobbyist

Van Scoyoc Associates, Maryland and Washington, D.C.

"You want to turn what your opponents think is an advantage to a disadvantage. In our fight against allowing slot machines in Maryland, we made money an issue. The gambling interests were pumping lots of money into the state, but we knew that if regular people heard about the money, they'd think, 'Those are bad guys.'"

arguments for supporting their positions. This information might be available for your casual perusal on-line. But be careful when doing on-line research. It is possible to find outrageous statements about any issue on-line, and you want to focus your efforts on those groups or individuals that have some credibility and visibility and are actively using grassroots or the news media to support their positions. Getting caught up in the obscure, outrageous arguments of extremists speaks more to the fact that there are kooks on-line than it helps address the real impact of your opposition.

TYPES OF OPPOSITION

Your opposition is not uniform or monolithic. It can come from many quarters when you are fighting for change. Here are some types of opposition that might spring up against your positions:

• Natural opposition. These are groups where there is a fundamental or ideological split between two distinct sides. You might never be able to work with or compromise on issues with your natural opposition. Prime examples of natural opponents are abortion (prochoice versus prolife groups) and gun control (pro-gun versus gun control groups).

• Fiscal opposition. This is opposition that does not have any sort of ideological split with your issue or cause but simply finds your solutions economically unattractive. Many of those who opposed adding a prescription drug benefit to Medicare did so because they were afraid that it was too expensive to be sustained, not because they did not want seniors to have access to medicine. Anti-tax advocates are likely to oppose any and all groups that advocate for increased government spending, despite how they personally feel about an issue. Different from natural opposition, fiscal opposition can sometimes be placated by demonstrating that the program you support provides tangible benefits, is not unreasonably expensive, and includes effective controls on the amount of money spent.

• Strange and unanticipated opposition. Sometimes the opposition seems to come out of left field. You may be an advocate for the National Association for School Lunches and find that the National Association of Wallpaper Stripping Contractors has a real problem with your piece of legislation. Legislation has a way of being amended as it wends its way through the process so that sometimes bills address many different issue areas and attract a motley crew of interested groups. This opposition is real even if it seems wacky. It has to be addressed, especially if your provisions will be lost if the overall bill is killed.

• Friendly fire. This is a common type of opposition that takes careful strategy and response to navigate. This is where a group that you are generally in line with opposes some specific bill that you support. In this situation, make sure that if you state your opposition, you do it in such a way that it does not jeopardize the beneficial relationship you usually enjoy with the group. Dealing with friendly fire requires maximum restraint.

HOW TO OPPOSE THE OPPOSITION

There are three basic steps to oppose the opposition:

Step 1: Acknowledge Their Arguments.

- Accurately and impersonally state any strong arguments that your opposition uses.

Step 2: Analyze Their Arguments

- Do they rely on emotional appeal?
- Are their statistics correctly stated?
- What legislators will respond to this argument?
- Are the news media attracted to this argument?

Step 3: Counteract Their Arguments

- Use a personal story.
- Question the statistics or research methods.
- Provide alternative statistics.
- Co-opt their concerns, but redirect the conclusions.
- Shift the basis of their argument to a more sympathetic aspect—for example, "This fight is about the children, not about the needs of big business."
- Dispassionately label the opposition as irrational, aggressive, and unfair if they objectively are.

If you know that your lawmaker is sympathetic to one of the arguments from your opposition, consider including one of your rebuttals in any letter, e-mail, or phone call you make related to a given bill.

If you are meeting face-to-face with your legislator and he disagrees with your position, try not to feel threatened. (Confrontations with a representative are relatively rare. Remember, representatives are inclined to try to please you.) Acknowledge his concern and then counteract it with one of the rebuttals you have prepared in your Preparing for the Opposition Worksheet

(Worksheet 7.1). For example, "I am aware that some local restaurants have spoken with you, Senator, about the potential impact of this legislation on their business. We are sensitive to those concerns, but other states that have adopted similar measures have experienced no adverse effects."

Remember that just because your opposition has arguments does not mean that your elected officials have heard them or that they have resonated in the legislative offices in the Capitol. You might strategically choose not to address any argument that the opposition has not itself effectively disseminated. Your job is to counter their effective arguments, not to help them make their case.

PART 2

Contact Your Elected Officials

Write an Effective Letter

In this chapter, you will learn:

- The power of a personalized letter
- What happens to a constituent letter in a legislative office
- If your letter should be typed or handwritten
- When you should refer to a proposed piece of legislation in your letter

Sometimes the classics are the best. When you are angry about something that the government has done or not done or might do, and your friends tell you to write a letter to your Congress member, you might think to yourself, *That's what we used to do in the old days. There must be some fundamental change in how we communicate with our elected officials now.*

In this case, the classic is still standing tall. A written letter—whether typed or handwritten—remains one of the most effective ways to communicate with your elected officials. The fact that so much communication these days takes place instantly over the phone or the Internet makes the written letter seem even more formal and charming.

WHAT HAPPENS TO A LETTER IN A LEGISLATIVE OFFICE

When you mail a written letter to a legislator, it is generally either counted (as a tally mark) or it is actually read and circulated by legislative staff—perhaps even given to your lawmaker. Your challenge is to make any letter you send read and circulated rather than simply counted.

Understanding what physically happens to letters in a typical congressional office will help you understand how to make the biggest impact on a legislator with your letters.

When you send a letter to a legislative office, the first thing that staff does (and it is usually staff) is look to see where the letter is from. The first question in their mind is not, *Does this letter present compelling arguments?* The first important question is, *Where does this person live?* If you do not live in the district, your letter very probably gets respectfully ignored.

Once staff has verified your address, they scan to see if your letter is a robot letter (prewritten or copied verbatim from an Action Alert) or if it has any original content. Robot letters tend to be merely counted. There is no original information provided about any of the senders aside from their name. Once you have read one, you've read them all.

The strategy of generating robot letters is to demonstrate that large numbers of voters support or oppose a specific bill. Counted letters and e-mail are duly reported to the lawmaker in a bill file (where staff collects all correspondence and analysis related to a particular bill) or in a bill memo (where correspondence and analysis are summarized in memo format). A bill memo might say, *We received 21 letters for S 123 and 211 against.* When it is time for the legislator to vote, he or she will see these tallies and probably interpret them as a rough barometer of how the district feels about the bill.

You might be able to go well beyond being counted if you write a personalized letter. Beyond demonstrating a broad base of support, robot letters tend to lack any specific detail—the kind of district-based information that lawmakers are interested in receiving from constituents. Furthermore, robot letters provide elected officials with little incentive to do more than vote the right way. It is difficult for them to make a floor speech on the issue or to discuss it with local news media if they don't have any specific examples that they can use. More than this, an individual letter from a constituent might make them care about the issue on a different level. Robot letters can demonstrate support, but it takes a personal local story to make a lawmaker care.

If your letter is unique—if it contains content about your life, your expertise, or the district in general—it might then be routed to the appropriate staffer who handles the issue that your letter addresses. On the state and local levels, staff might be nonexistent, and your letter might be presented directly to the elected official. In any case, a personalized letter that gets noticed in a legislative office is poised to have a solid impact.

Now, as always with grassroots, if you are participating in an organized grassroots action as a result of an Action Alert, you have to stay on message, which means your request has to be exactly the same as everybody else who is writing. By personalized, I mean that you explain your request with a local example: you share either a personal story from your own life or your professional expertise as a local resident—a doctor who works at a local hospital, for example, or a local small business owner. There is no guarantee that a personalized letter will make it to the lawmaker's desk, but the chances tend to be favorable. Most lawmakers are genuinely interested in getting solid, local information from the district. (See Illustration 2.1 in Action 2.)

One-Hour Rule

Never send a robot letter copied verbatim from an Action Alert. Always individualize your letters to elected officials with examples from your personal life, your professional life, or your community.

Elected officials generally like to respond to their constituents who take the time to send personalized letters—even robot letters from constituents tend to get replies from the legislative offices. Because your elected officials must respond to inquiries about every issue out there, they usually rely on form letters that thank you for sharing your views and assure you that the lawmaker will take your views under consideration, especially if you send a robot letter. If you send a personalized letter, you will sometimes get back a personalized response from your lawmaker, letting you know that the lawmaker did in fact read your letter and take it seriously.

WHAT IF I DON'T HAVE TIME TO INDIVIDUALIZE MY LETTER?

For issues that truly matter to you, it should not be too much of a sacrifice to spend an hour composing a personalized letter to your elected officials a few times a year. However, robot letters are better than no communication at all. The tallies they generate give lawmakers a snapshot of the district—a limited, unscientific poll that lets the lawmaker know that people in the district care about a pending piece of legislation. At the same time,

Advice from the Field

Carlea Bauman

National Director of Grassroots Advocacy

American Diabetes Association

"Human drama is more interesting than cold statistics. If you're trying to make a point on an issue, tell your elected official about how your life has been affected by it. Which of the following statements is more powerful? 'Millions of people have diabetes in the United States' or 'My son was diagnosed with diabetes at age five. Since then, I have watched him receive over 10,000 shots of insulin.'"

you are leaving to chance that someone else in your district—someone who feels exactly the opposite of the way you do on a given issue—will communicate in a more substantive way on the issue, perhaps securing a gut-level commitment from the lawmaker that will not effectively be countered by tally marks from robot letters from your side.

COMMON QUESTIONS ABOUT WRITING TO ELECTED OFFICIALS

Unsure of how to proceed when you write to your elected officials? The following answers to common questions will help to guide you:

• Am I still allowed to mail a written letter to my representatives these days? Some people think that because several letters containing anthrax were mailed to U.S. Senate offices in the fall of 2001 that you can no longer mail letters to your elected officials. This is *not* true. You can absolutely send a letter by U.S. mail to your elected officials at every level of government. However, letters to Congress might take several days longer to arrive due to increased security measures. Your only consideration is if your window of opportunity on a given bill is sufficient to accommodate a few weeks or so of transit time for a mailed letter to your representative or senators.

• Typed or handwritten? Some legislative offices say that they place more importance on a handwritten letter, but few actually make such a distinction. If you opt for the handwritten letter, make sure your handwriting is legible. Alternatively, feel free to use your computer to compose, spell-check, and print out a typed letter to be mailed by the U.S. Postal Service. The choice is yours.

• Should I discuss the legislative process or focus on the issues? Avoid wasting your precious space on discussions about the legislative process, the mechanics of introducing amendments, how to get around a filibuster, and so forth. That is the job of your elected officials, and they are fully capable of navigating the legislative process without your input. It is enough for you to express support or opposition to a bill and let your lawmaker figure out how to shepherd it through the Congress or state house.

• Send your letter to the district office or the Capitol? A letter on current bills might make it to the appropriate staff a little more quickly if you send it to the Capitol, but your lawmakers should be efficiently routing all correspondence no matter where it is received.

• Send a letter or a fax? There was a time when legislative staff were annoyed by the constituent letter that came over the fax machine, but now the fax has become the preferred method of communication for some offices. If your legislative office accepts faxes from constituents, feel free to communicate this way. If your local lawmakers say that they would rather not have you use the fax machine to communicate with the office, respect their request.

TIPS FOR COMPOSING AN EFFECTIVE LETTER TO YOUR REPRESENTATIVES

Some do's and don'ts will help you write an effective letter, as will the sample letter in Example 8.1.

Do

- Do address your lawmaker as "The Honorable," even if you don't think he or she is.

- Do address the lawmaker by the correct title (for example, Senator Snow or Representative Smith).

- Do state that you are a constituent and provide the street address where you live at the beginning of any piece of correspondence. This is critical: lawmakers are under no real obligation to consider the requests of citizens who are not their constituents.

- Do state your opposition to or support for a bill by bill number early in the letter. This will help clarify your position and aid in routing your letter to the correct staff and/or the correct bill file.

- Do personalize your letter. Don't get so caught up in explaining the legislation or providing local statistics that you forget to talk about your life, your family, your job, and your neighborhood.

Example 8.1. Sample Letter to a Representative

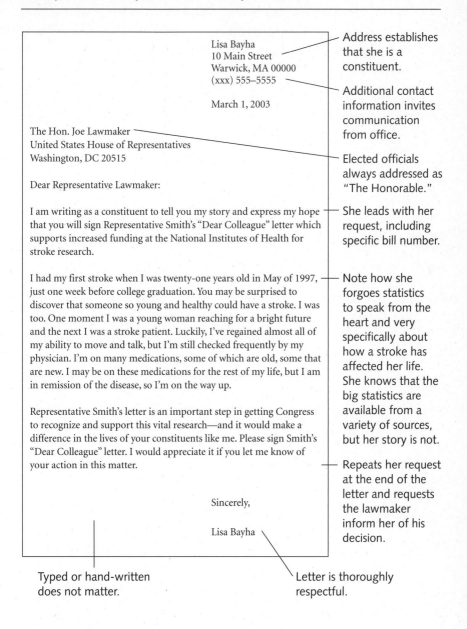

Lisa Bayha
10 Main Street
Warwick, MA 00000
(xxx) 555–5555

Address establishes that she is a constituent.

Additional contact information invites communication from office.

March 1, 2003

The Hon. Joe Lawmaker
United States House of Representatives
Washington, DC 20515

Elected officials always addressed as "The Honorable."

Dear Representative Lawmaker:

I am writing as a constituent to tell you my story and express my hope that you will sign Representative Smith's "Dear Colleague" letter which supports increased funding at the National Institutes of Health for stroke research.

She leads with her request, including specific bill number.

I had my first stroke when I was twenty-one years old in May of 1997, just one week before college graduation. You may be surprised to discover that someone so young and healthy could have a stroke. I was too. One moment I was a young woman reaching for a bright future and the next I was a stroke patient. Luckily, I've regained almost all of my ability to move and talk, but I'm still checked frequently by my physician. I'm on many medications, some of which are old, some that are new. I may be on these medications for the rest of my life, but I am in remission of the disease, so I'm on the way up.

Note how she forgoes statistics to speak from the heart and very specifically about how a stroke has affected her life. She knows that the big statistics are available from a variety of sources, but her story is not.

Representative Smith's letter is an important step in getting Congress to recognize and support this vital research—and it would make a difference in the lives of your constituents like me. Please sign Smith's "Dear Colleague" letter. I would appreciate it if you let me know of your action in this matter.

Repeats her request at the end of the letter and requests the lawmaker inform her of his decision.

Sincerely,

Lisa Bayha

Typed or hand-written does not matter.

Letter is thoroughly respectful.

- Do be brief. Two typed pages is an unofficial maximum for written letters to an elected official, but shorter is better. After you state your position, provide a few sentences or paragraphs of justification, and then politely end your letter. Excess rhetoric or meandering stories will detract from your request.

- Do repeat your request at the end of the letter. As with any other exercise in communication, repeating the most important part of your message helps it stick.

- Do send a copy of your letter to the interest group that sent you an Action Alert on the topic. Copies of such letters helps gauge the overall success of a given grassroots campaign.

Don't

- Don't copy sample letters from your political group or association verbatim (but remember that you want to stay on message by making the exact same request as everyone else who is writing on the same issue) It is especially egregious to photocopy sample letters and mail them to lawmakers. Such laziness might convey a lack of serious commitment on your behalf. Sample letters should be personalized and rewritten in your own hand or retyped on your computer.

- Don't assume that only staff will see your letter. Especially at the state and local levels of government, your legislator might open and process her own mail, so write your letter as if you are speaking directly to her.

- Don't provide extensive clippings, articles, studies, or material you have printed off the Internet. Legislative offices do not have room to file extensive amounts of paper from any one constituent, and they will almost certainly not have the time necessary to read the extras you have sent. If there is a particularly interesting study or article you wish to reference, mention it in the body of your letter, and offer to supply a copy upon request.

- Don't be condescending, degrading, sarcastic, threatening, or dismissive. No one wants to help someone who does not treat them with respect, and a letter is a poor medium for intimidation. Never assume, through your rhetoric, that your legislators are dishonest, disinterested, or incompetent. Every letter you write is an opportunity to broaden your relationship with your lawmakers and deepen their understanding of your issues, even if they do not totally agree with your positions. A snotty or threatening letter tends to close that door forever.

- Don't argue every point that comes to mind. You will end up writing far too long a letter. Let your lawmakers know only the few arguments that are most important to you.

- Don't offer ultimatums. The American policy process is fraught with compromises. Compromise is not necessarily an indication of a legislative defeat. In almost all cases, it is a mark of victory. Don't threaten to withdraw support if legislation you care about is amended as it wends its way through the process. There are, of course, limits, but you want to convey that you (and the interest groups that represent your interests) are willing to be reasonably flexible.

- Don't lie or exaggerate. If you think you can pull a big one over on a career politician or his or her staff, think again. Letters that are just plain unbelievable do not motivate your representatives to carry a torch for you. Quite the opposite: such letters will make them wary of supporting you, and seasoned legislators can smell outrageous exaggerations when they open your envelope.

- Don't procrastinate. Bills must survive numerous votes to become law, and they need grassroots support every step of the way. Don't wait to send your letter.

- Don't say that because you made a campaign contribution, you expect the legislator to vote a certain way. This sounds like bribery, which is illegal, and it will likely have the effect of getting a lawmaker to distance himself from your issue rather than embrace it.

WHAT IF MY ELECTED OFFICIAL DISAGREES WITH ME?

Chances are that your elected officials will be loathe to pick a fight with you over any issue. Advocates who storm Capitol Hill expecting to get in heated arguments or pointed debates with the powers that be are often sorely disappointed.

About the last thing that your representatives want to do to an actual voter from the district is to make you upset or angry. Still, any vote on a bill will have winners and losers, and advocates should be wary of being placated by a representative who has no intention of ever voting their way. So how can you tell if you really got through to them or if they just don't care?

Every now and then, you will encounter a lawmaker who is honest and forthright and will explain to you how she really feels—that is, why she might disagree with your position or be inclined to seek an alternative solution to a problem that you are both concerned about. There are many advocates who are often terrified of such honesty, but I always encourage them to welcome those exchanges. If nothing else, it is worth noting if you have a legislator who has the backbone to share unpleasant truths with you (as long as the person is polite when expressing disagreement).

"Thank you for sharing" is one of those generic legislative replies that is always appropriate but sometimes is used as a mask to hide behind for those legislators who do not support your position but don't think it's worth getting into an argument about.

The thank-you-for-sharing response does not automatically mean that your lawmaker is in complete disagreement with you. Legislators are often noncommittal. They don't like to announce a position until they have heard from all sides and until they get a sense of what the broader politics that surround a given issue are going to be. Once they vote, however, you've got them. No matter how much equivocating he does on his official Web site or in the press, once your lawmaker has voted, he has either helped your cause or not helped it, and you are entitled to an explanation.

If your representative does not vote your way on a given issue, consider the following:

• Did you write a letter, call, or meet with your elected official before the vote? If not, you have no right to be angry. Your lawmakers are not psychics. If you have not initiated a substantive exchange with the official on the issues you care about, you cannot assume that he will vote as if he knows your life experiences, your insights, your struggles, and your passions.

• Take a deep breath, and get some perspective. No matter how much you convince yourself that the bill in question would lead to world peace, love, and harmony or, alternatively, Armageddon, now is the time to come back down to earth and realize that you win some and you lose some. You still have your family, your life, and your other passions besides politics. You may not be happy, you may need to regroup, your interest group may need to pursue an alternative strategy, you may need to turn up the heat on your individual representatives to see if you can get them to be a little more helpful, but don't go off the deep end.

• Do they vote your way on most issues? No lawmaker will likely vote the way you want her to 100 percent of the time. So take into account if your representative usually votes your way on the issues you care about, and this one issue represents an occasional anomaly. This does not stop you

Internet Tip

For House and Senate mailing addresses, go to the House and Senate Web sites—respectively, http://www.house.gov and http://www.senate.gov.

For state and local mailing addresses, check out state and local Web sites or go to the State and Local Government Internet Resource Page: http://www.loc.gov/global/state/stategov.html

from urging her to take a different position on the bill in question or from politely expressing your disappointment after she has voted, but you should carefully consider how much anger you want to convey. It is probably not worth it to undermine an otherwise functional relationship for the occasional disappointment.

• Did you weaken her resolve on the issue? Your lawmakers might never, ever support the issues you care about, but your efforts can at least keep them from being champions for your opposition. Make it clear that there is thoughtful and respectful opposition to your lawmaker's positions, and she will think carefully about the possible consequences every time she votes. Sometimes you can even get a lawmaker who does not support your position on a bill to simply not vote on it. She does not help you—but she does not help the other side either. Such actions can be significant strategic gains because they help undermine the power of your opposition.

• Is this somebody you just can't reach? If you have tried to communicate with your elected official, shared your stories and expertise, you may find that no matter how many times you meet with her or write to her, she not only votes the opposite you would have her do but seems to actually enjoy it. Sometimes, your lawmaker will truly be a lost cause on the issues you care about. This is the kind of legislator whom you have to meet on Election Day in the voting booth. There is no question that some elected officials are better out of office as far as your issue area is concerned. But be sure that you have a hopeless case before you completely write off any of your representatives.

Send a Powerful E-Mail

In this chapter, you will learn:

- The first thing you should mention in any e-mail to an elected official
- Why you should alter any pre-written e-mail message provided by an on-line interest group.
- Why sending e-mail is not always as good as a snail mail letter
- Why you should not send e-mail to a number of lawmakers at the same time.

The Internet came along, and it was good—good for shopping (especially for books). And it was good for bidding on things, strange things, hard-to-get things, collectible things. It was also a really great place to chat with people you did not know. It was a really great place to do research, virtually giving people the contents of a huge public library at their fingertips. The Internet was also good for sending messages in the form of e-mail. Another thing that the Internet was supposed to be good at—but that remains to be seen—is democracy, especially grassroots advocacy.

We were told that American citizens would be put in touch with their government in a way that heretofore was never dreamed of. Citizens who were worried about one of the many issues of the day could simply go on-line and, with little or no effort, let legislators know how they felt about that issue. Petitions, those old stalwarts of democratic expression, found new life on the Internet—and seemed a brand new way to have an impact on the legislative process. Americans were now able to gather thousands, even millions, of signatures on e-mail with little or no effort by using the Internet.

The central organizing principle of much of on-line grassroots tools seems to be the ease with which the Internet makes communication possible. The Internet can reduce communication with your elected officials to a single mouse click or two. And . . . somehow it has been found wanting.

CHOOSE E-MAIL CAREFULLY

The supreme ethos espoused by all things Internet is speed, but speed in an advocacy context can signal lack of investment, lack of careful thought, the very limitations of low-impact grassroots. When you stop to think about it, why would American citizens who care passionately about a pending issue find it satisfying to reduce their commitment, their insight, their need to express themselves to a prewritten e-mail that merely involves a few clicks of the mouse? Most people are drawn to issues because their lives have been personally affected by them or because their expertise has given them a nuanced insight. Yet the Internet, that transforming communications tool, tends to disfavor political substance for ease and speed.

Perhaps the biggest price we have paid is that this misplaced enthusiasm has distracted people unnecessarily from the historic advantages to concerned citizens that the Internet does in fact afford, which have gone generally unheralded. In my book *Cybercitizen,* I informed advocates about some of the truly ground-breaking and empowering informational resources that the Internet provides. Access to voting records, text of pending legislation, campaign finance reports, news media search engines, even basic districting information are all unprecedented resources that the Internet has made available for Americans who know how to use them.

As for quick-click e-mails to your elected officials with prewritten messages, their value is dubious. Most legislative offices tend to ascribe a level of value to grassroots communications depending on how much effort they take. An e-mail that takes about two seconds to send arrives in a legislative office with the unfortunate impression that while you may care about an issue, you probably care about the issue only in passing. There is no indication whether you possess any local insights or any compelling stories that argue on a visceral level for the commitment of a given elected official to your request. Quick and easy e-mail interfaces do not provide any indication to the elected official that the sender will have any idea or care come election time how the representative voted.

Electronic petitions are even worse. They may be easy to distribute. They may be fat with names and e-mail addresses, but what legislative office can pull out the bona-fide constituents from such a document? And remember, until your legislator can identify a constituent, she is not available to be persuaded.

Being counted is not the same thing as creating a sense of urgency around an issue. Generating e-mail is not the same as illustrating how a proposed piece of legislation will play out for the particular constituents living in a particular district represented by a particular lawmaker. On-line technology, which has forever altered so much of our world, has not changed the basics of grassroots advocacy. The same things that make a personalized letter better than a postcard apply to e-mail, and perhaps even more. By using the computer to communicate with your elected officials, you are, from the start, fighting against a medium that appears to be too quick and too easy to express the sentiments of those who really care about an issue.

Yet things are evolving at a rapid rate, and legislative offices are increasingly becoming more comfortable with e-mail and more savvy about discerning the origins of the e-mail they receive. Virtually all elected officials in the United States now have e-mail addresses, and a great many maintain individual Web sites. Some lawmakers even encourage their constituents to communicate with their offices using e-mail. So, it's not that sending e-mail to your lawmakers is necessarily a bad thing to do. The point is that there are better and worse ways to send e-mail.

An on-line interface is fine if it allows you to customize any message you send with a few lines where you can explain who you are, why you care, or how you see a proposed piece of legislation affecting the district. Avoid using a Web site that reduces your input and identity on any issue to a cookie-cutter, prewritten statement with no ability to incorporate your personal stories or local arguments. If you can insert your personal insights into a prewritten e-mail, make sure you do so. Alternatively, you can always opt to send a more personal letter, even if a grassroots network you belong to has provided an on-line interface.

TIPS FOR SENDING EFFECTIVE E-MAIL

The main thing to keep in mind if you choose to share your thoughts using e-mail is that you must provide your voting address as the *very first line* in your e-mail. You might even put your address as part of the e-mail subject header.

If you use an interface provided by an organized interest group you will no doubt notice that the first piece of information these interfaces ask you for is your mailing address. Similarly, many elected officials provide on-line forms that you can fill out as a way to communicate with their office on-line. Some offices, in fact, will accept your on-line input only if you use their interface. Those interfaces will solicit your mailing address.

If you feel that you must protect your privacy by not disclosing to an elected official where you live, the chances are they will not be reading your e-mail.

As you can imagine, legislative offices get an enormous amount of junk e-mail every day, and there is probably an intern in the office whose job it is to tear through the e-mail and delete anything that is not from a constituent. Any e-mail that does not clearly demonstrate that it is being

One-Hour Rule
It is imperative that any e-mail from you screams "constituent"! Make sure your voting address is the very first line of any e-mail you send to your representative.

sent by a constituent from the district seriously runs the risk of deletion without being read.

Here are ways to make e-mail work for you (Example 9.1 shows a sample e-mail message):

Example 9.1. A Powerful E-Mail Message

To: e-mail@joerepresentative.house.gov.

Re: Request from Warwick

My name is Lisa Bayha. I am a constituent who lives at 10 Main Street in Warwick, RI, 00000.

I am writing as a constituent to tell you my story and express my hope that you will sign Representative Smith's "Dear Colleague" letter which supports the need for increased funding at the National Institutes of Health for stroke research.

I had my first stroke when I was twenty-one years old, and medical research is the main reason why I have been able to recover as fully as I have. Although I have had a promising recovery (thanks, in part, to the excellent medical staff at Potomac General), I am still on many medications—some of them new. I may have to rely on these medications for the rest of my life.

I sent this e-mail with the hope that you will understand that stroke research is truly helping your constituents at home. Again, please sign the Smith "Dear Colleague" letter.

Thank you.

With e-mail, it is even more important that you signal your constituent status early.

She opens her e-mail with her mailing address to signal she is a constituent but also to provide a way to respond (many legislative offices will only respond by snail mail).

The success of the e-mail will be determined by the personalized local information it conveys.

Note: The text is very similar to that of a mailed letter.

Do

- Do put your name and address at the top of every message so staff can identify you as a constituent. You might even consider putting your name and address in the subject line so it is the first thing read.

- Do personalize your e-mail. Customize any e-mail that is provided by an interest group with your own personal stories and local statistics. Create a unique message even if you are participating in a larger action on-line (but remember to keep the request exactly as it is provided to stay on message.)

- Do be brief. There is not a lot of patience among lawmakers or their staff for scrolling down through lengthy e-mails. Make sure your e-mail is personalized, but you probably do not have more than a few paragraphs to get the job done.

- Do be clear about your request. You do not want your lawmaker to simply care about a given issue—you want her to take a specific action on that issue. If you write to your federal elected officials, your e-mail is likely to be circulated among staff. Make it absolutely clear what your request is (and if you are sending e-mail as part of a coordinated interest group campaign, stay on message). A good idea is to begin and end your e-mail with a statement of your request.

- Do proofread your e-mail. We get going so fast writing e-mail that on-line messages are often riddled with grammatical errors and spelling mistakes. This kind of sloppiness will detract from the urgency of your request. (Don't go into meltdown if you discover a minor typo later. Your personal story should still carry the day.)

- Do consider establishing a relationship with your legislator through a face-to-face meeting before beginning to send e-mail (see Action 16). E-mail can be an extremely timely and powerful way for you to communicate with your local legislative offices after they have met you and recognize you as a voter from the district with important insights on an issue. Once they know who you are, your e-mail has a much better chance of commanding more than a cursory glance by the intern.

- Don't flame. It is easy to dehumanize the person on the receiving end of your e-mail, especially if you have never met her, and she is a politician. Real people with real feelings will read your e-mail, and they might even be people who would champion your issue if you only make a polite request.

- Don't spam. Avoid any tendency to attach files to your lawmakers. It is a rare day when such attachments are read. Your job is to explain

Advice from the Field

Stephanie Vance

Advocacy guru

AdVanced Consulting

"Congressional offices are beginning to use software to help them deal with the flood of e-mail they get every day. An emerging tool scans incoming e-mail for identical messages—prewritten messages obviously sent with a minimum of input from the constituent. Some offices can now route this e-mail to a folder where it is easy to send a form letter response with a minimum of effort from the legislator. A better way is to send an original e-mail that might make the same request but in a more personal, thoughtful manner. These messages are much less likely to be filtered out."

Send a Powerful E-Mail

why you as a voting constituent care about a specific issue. Your job is not to find, copy, and send every file on the Internet related to an issue you care about.

- Don't send messages too often. Be careful about sending an e-mail on every issue that you hear about. If you end up trying to communicate with your elected officials too often, they will lose sight of the issues that you really care about and will not be able to discern the areas in which you have personal experiences or professional expertise.

- Don't send your e-mail at odd hours, like 2:00 A.M. There are legislative staffers who notice the time when e-mail is sent and are wary of e-mail sent in the dead of night. If this is a good time for you to compose e-mails have your browser send them in the morning during regular business hours.

- Don't send copies (cc) to anybody. If you are asking an elected official to do something important on your behalf, make sure that you are asking him and only him for his valuable assistance. Never send your e-mail to every member of the U.S. government no matter how awesome you think your arguments are. Remember: if you are not a voter, they probably will not care. Even if you plan to send a similar e-mail to both of your U.S. senators, make sure you send them individually. You are much more likely to get a serious response.

Internet Tip

Most elected officials have e-mail addresses and interactive on-line forms to facilitate e-mail exchanges with their constituents.

Make a Compelling Phone Call

In this chapter, you will learn:

- What an effective phone call sounds like
- What happens when you call an elected official's office
- When it is better to call a legislative office rather than send a letter
- If it matters who you speak to in a legislative office

A phone call to an elected official is a relatively cheap and instant way to share what is on your mind. By now, you should see low-impact warning flags go up when you see the word *instant* in close proximity to any grassroots action. We know instant forms of grassroots communication tend to be limited because they tend to discourage individual local information from the sender—usually the most compelling thing that an advocate has to share. Still, a well-timed phone call to a legislative office does have its uses.

First, let's talk about what to expect. You are allowed to call your representatives, and while it may be a little difficult to get your actual representative on the horn, staff generally welcome reasonable phone calls from constituents.

The White House puts you into a glorified answering machine called the comment line where you can use the buttons on your phone to register your opinion (again, not exactly the same as being able to tell your personal story). When you call your representatives at the federal, state, and local levels of government, you are likely to get a breathing, talking person on the other end—and sometimes you will, in fact, get the lawmaker.

When a phone call comes into a legislative office, the staff (or member) is initially interested in one thing: where you are calling from. That is, are you a constituent? It is a mistake to launch into your personal story without first explaining who you are and where you live. If you are a constituent, you have their ear.

You do not need to be able to quote the proposed piece of legislation word for word. A simple statement of whether you support or oppose a proposed piece of legislation and a sentence or two about why is sufficient.

The ephemeral nature of a phone call makes it difficult to allot more than a minute or two for any particular phone call to a legislative office, so the exchanges tend to be quite brief. Be prepared for this.

Strategically, any phone calls that come into a legislative office are likely to be tallied. Staff will probably not have time to take down your personal story. If you have a compelling individual story, you'll want to seriously consider a text-based form of communication (letters or e-mail) before you avail yourself of the convenience of a brief phone call to a legislative office. A phone call can effectively express support or opposition to a proposed piece of legislation, but any additional information is likely to get lost.

That being said, when time is at a premium, a phone call might be the best way to communicate with a legislative office. You can catch the House debating something you care about on C-SPAN and make a call before the speaker on the floor finishes.

There is a way to boost the power of your phone calls. Sometimes if you have met your lawmaker or staff by participating in a face-to-face meeting (see Action 16), you will have established a relationship, and the member or staff will take your calls personally, effectively getting you past the receptionist and off the tally page. This puts you in the enviable position of being able to substantively communicate with the legislative offices by providing local arguments and examples of why you want them to support or oppose a particular piece of legislation.

LIMITATIONS AND ADVANTAGES OF MAKING GRASS-ROOTS PHONE CALLS

Phone calls do have limitations. They tend to be so brief that they cannot convey much personal or district-based information. Moreover, unlike a personal letter, phone calls to a legislative office overwhelmingly tend to be tallied. Local details provided in such phone calls are difficult to transfer between staff. A written letter or e-mail keeps your stories or arguments perfectly intact as it is passed from staffer to legislator.

In spite of their limitations, the speed and convenience of phone calls in some cases provide a tremendous advantage. When the bill you care about is currently being debated on the floor of the House or Senate, it may be too late to send a letter, but it is not too late to call your lawmakers. A lawmaker who receives a flood of phone calls before a vote gets the impression that people in the district are watching, that she better carefully consider her vote, and that there will be consequences to her actions on this particular bill.

A strategic consideration when you rely on a phone call to make your point is your opposition's ability to retaliate in a similar fashion. If you are going to be reduced to a single tally mark, you want to be sure that your side has more tallies than your

One-Hour Rule

Phone calls are best used when time is of the essence—when a bill is in the process of being debated and voted on and a more substantive method of communication would arrive too late to make a difference.

opposition. If you live by the game of numbers, you will die by the numbers if your opposition is more active. If you find yourself on the losing side of a lopsided battle with your opposition, take the time to send a thoughtful letter or to schedule an in-person meeting with your representative. One compelling, local, personal story can trump a slew of nameless, faceless tallies.

Sometimes, you may choose to make a phone call on an issue that has been extensively covered in the news media to the point where you are certain that your elected officials have heard all of the possible arguments related to an issue and would not benefit from any additional elaboration of the arguments. In such a situation, you may just want to be counted but not feel the need to rehash the arguments. Be careful not to sell yourself short in this regard. Remember that a particularly vivid personal story is always useful, especially if it helps bolster your position.

Sometimes political groups use phone calls to stage peaceful protests by having so many people call in at one time that they effectively para-

Advice from the Field

John Goodwin

Grassroots Outreach Coordinator

Humane Society of the United States

"An effective phone call is concise yet gets the message across. Mention the issue, bill number, and your position. Be civil and avoid the tendency to ramble."

lyze the legislative office. This is a way that groups can punish elected officials they feel are doing harm or as a way to force open channels of communication that have been closed. Often called *phone zaps,* they are sure to get the lawmaker's attention if they are done effectively. But this sort of thing can backfire and make your lawmaker an enemy for life. Most elected officials are less than thrilled at having their business machines commandeered. You must weigh the moral imperative of the issue at hand against the possible negative consequences before you participate in a phone zap.

ADVICE ON THE PHONE CALL

Here are ways to make your phone call work (Example 10.1 gives a sample script):

Do

- Do state your name and home address as a way of establishing that you are a constituent.

- Do clearly state your position and refer to a bill by its official number— for example, "I would like Senator Jones to vote in support of SB 6." If you would like to suggest amendments or a more complicated position that requires explanation, you should opt for a written letter. Keep in mind that if you are calling as part of an organized effort of a grassroots network you belong to, that you must stay on message—your request must be exactly the same as everyone else who is calling as part of that Action Alert.

- Do request a response. This lets the office know that you are serious about your request and just might be watching when the vote is taken.

- Do establish a relationship with the legislative office before relying on phone communication. Set up a face-to-face meeting with the legislator as a way to establish who you are and why you care about an issue.

Example 10.1. Sample Phone Call Script

Hello, my name is Colleen Stack. I am a constituent from Kansas City.

Staff: Thanks for calling. What is your mailing address?

My mailing address is 10 Main Street, Kansas City, 00000. —— She leads with her address to let them know she is a constituent.

Staff: Great. And how can we help you?

I am calling to ask for my representative's support of HR 1234, a bill that would increase our commitment to epilepsy research at the National Institutes of Health. —— She gets right to the request, including specific bill number and requested action.

Staff: Okay.

I am the mother of a young adult with epilepsy. You know, there is incredible research going on. It's just amazing how far we've come—the number of medications that are available and the technology. My daughter is a living testament to what we've been able to accomplish. —— She has very limited time, so she briefly presents the human side of the issue (and the local angle).

Staff: Thanks for sharing your views. I will let the member know.

Thanks so much, and could someone call me and let me know how she voted on HR 1234? —— She requests follow-up information to let them know she will continue to follow the issue.

Staff: It would probably be easier if you called the health legislative assistant, Melissa Wong, in a few weeks, and she will let you know. —— She can begin to build a professional relationship with the right staff person now that she has a name.

Thanks again.

She is unfailingly polite throughout the exchange.

If the legislator or staff knows you personally, you might be able to get off the tally page and leave a more substantive message.

- Do call during business hours. Leaving a message on an answering machine is a bit dicey in terms of being sure that your opinion is properly recorded.

Don't

- Don't worry whether you should call the district office or the Capitol. Staff should be able to record your sentiments in either location. If you want to save a long-distance charge of a call to Washington, then use the local office to leave your comment. If you have a relationship with a particular staffer, it is probably best to call the office that person works in (most staff do not work in all of a legislator's offices.)

- Don't try to get the legislator on the phone in person. If the legislator or her legislative assistants are not available, then graciously allow the receptionist to record your comment.

- Don't take up more than a minute of the staff's time. Unless you have previously established a relationship with a staffer, your phone message is likely to get translated into a tally mark, no matter what you say. If you find that the nature of a phone call precludes you from relating an important argument or story, then write and send a detailed letter.

- Don't be threatening, discourteous, or snide. The same etiquette imperatives that apply to sending a personal letter also apply here.

- Don't read a suggested phone script verbatim. If you are making a phone call as part of an Action Alert from an interest group, do not simply read a phone script verbatim. Memorize the request, and then put the script away. You are not a robot, and you should not imitate one when you phone your legislators.

- Don't call and give your opinion on every issue being debated on C-SPAN. You want your legislator to know which issues are most important to you, and it is presumptuous to suggest that he will need your guidance for every single bill he has to vote on. If you feel such a need to share, run for public office. If you win, you can personally vote on every single issue.

- Don't call and say that because you made a campaign contribution, you demand your legislator vote a certain way. This sounds like bribery, which is illegal, and it will likely have the effect of getting a lawmaker to distance himself from your issue rather than embrace it.

ACTION 11

Persuade Others to Act

In this chapter, you will learn:

- Why grassroots organizing succeeds one person at a time, even with the communications technology now available
- The best people to approach about embracing your cause
- Examples of what you can do to get others to take action

As any honest marketing executive will tell you, word-of-mouth is still the best, most reliable, most coveted method of getting people to purchase a new product, read a book, see a movie, or, for that matter, participate in a grassroots Action Alert. Forget the multimillion dollar ad campaigns and the technological wizardry of the Internet. Word-of-mouth remains one of the most powerful methods of communication in the United States.

Once you have personally mastered the advocacy tools outlined in this book—selecting your issues, identifying current legislation related to those issues, supporting or opposing legislation with your local stories and statistics, and communicating effectively with your elected officials—you can use those same skills to lobby your friends, family members, local organizations, clubs, and civic groups to build up the number of local, vocal advocates who stand up to be counted on the issues you care about.

Let's start with the easiest prospects. In most cases, your family relationships are long established, amicable, and in general agreement on political issues—not always, mind you; if you often argue about current issues or political parties, you will want to skip your family and find advocates elsewhere. For the family of like-minded political thinkers what easier place than the dinner table to turn one letter into five and one e-mail message into ten?

Once you have exhausted your family possibilities, think of gathering with friends, your coworkers (but be careful of distracting anyone from their work to engage in politics on the clock), local clubs and organizations, and other gatherings. People who share your views will often enthusiastically welcome suggestions for how they too can really make a difference. You will not automatically find advocates in all of these locations, but they do generally represent the sphere of people you have personal contact with—and that is the sphere where you will experience the most success as far as grassroots recruitment is concerned.

ADVICE ON PERSUADING OTHERS TO JOIN THE FIGHT

Here are some tips to keep in mind when persuading others to take action.

Think Small, Very Small

Just as a bag of identical postcards or a slew of carbon copy e-mails fails to make a strong impression on your elected officials, your efforts to spread the word should focus on individuals rather than mere numbers. If one friend feels the same way about a candidate that you do but is not planning on voting on Election Day, give him or her a ride to the polls. In the same way, a couple of thoughtful letters can have a significant impact on the thinking of an elected official. Successfully escorting a friend through the process of writing a letter to an elected official is well worth your time.

Reach Out for the Most Obvious Supporters

Advocates often make a critical mistake when they attempt to mobilize their communities. They assume everyone in their community should be just as concerned about their issues as they are. This is seldom true. Individuals tend to care about narrow bands of issues that they have a gut-level reaction to. Don't spend your time pursuing every single group that meets regularly in your neighborhood; focus on those that have a similar interest to the one you are concerned about—that is, groups you belong to and groups where you already have friendly or professional relationships established.

There is no need to chase down every single limb on your family tree. If your uncle does not ever see things your way politically, don't strain your relationship over politics; simply focus on your aunt, who is more enlightened.

Provide a Simple, Concrete Action for New Recruits to Take

It is important that you communicate to potential advocates that they can make a difference if they become politically active but avoid presenting them with an open-ended list of possible actions to take. Have them start by writing their own version of the most recent letter or e-mail that you sent. Share your version, and encourage them to make it their own (while staying on message). You might then tell them about an interest group you belong to or help them sign up for a grassroots network you belong to. Escorting them through their initial piece of communication helps tremendously in creating a confident active advocate; it's usually not enough to just send someone an on-line link to your interest group.

Encourage Them from the Beginning to Personalize Any Communication with Their Elected Officials

Don't try to make it sound as if being politically active takes no time, effort, or thought at all. This is a very common pitfall of grassroots recruitment; we are so concerned with people's busy schedules that we try to tell people that their heartfelt political opinions can effectively be relegated to a few clicks of a mouse and require no serious time commitment. You want to encourage new advocates to engage in high-impact grassroots communications, and if they are truly interested in the issue, they will welcome the invitation to play a substantive role in the fight.

Avoid Hyperbole

A lot of us are nervous speaking in front of groups, even small ones. Others of us are so emotional about the issues that we care about that we become easily flustered. Sometimes our command of the technical aspects of their issues is limited. In all of these cases, it is tempting to resort to exaggeration to compensate for our insecurities. Just as assuming that you need to mobilize others by the millions to be effective is a misconception, making every issue seem like a life-or-death situation will make people wary of you. You may be able to work some people who don't deeply understand your issue into a panic, but they will not fool your elected officials. The worst part is that if your advocates find that they were misinformed or duped, they might not give grassroots advocacy another chance.

Listen to Their Priorities

People might support your position for reasons other than your own. A multifaceted commitment to an issue bolsters your position in the long run, so listen to potential advocates when they explain the aspects of their interest or voice concerns about proposed bills or candidates. Facilitate any requests for more information by connecting them with your interest groups or providing background reading yourself. If a group cannot support you on the current issue but might on a future issue, be polite, acknowledge your differences, and keep the channels of communication open. You will be glad you did.

Try Not to Take Rejection Personally

Be prepared for rejection. Some people will tell you that they do not want to become involved no matter how important you feel that your issue is. Sometimes rejection is a good thing. You do not want people to be nice to your face without any intention of writing a single letter or making a single campaign contribution. Allow people who are not interested to decline your invitation to advocacy. Don't browbeat them, and don't ruin any family or business relationships over it.

Rejection is hard, but recognizing that a certain amount of rejection is inevitable while recruiting others will help prevent rejection from immobilizing you. There is always another advocate waiting to be discovered, and you want to make sure you don't stop seeking others who might actively support your position just because a few along the way will not become involved.

Mind Your Etiquette

All of the same rules about being polite, honest, focused, and sincere that apply to other advocacy actions apply here too.

OPPORTUNITIES TO PERSUADE OTHERS TO TAKE ACTION

Always be on the lookout for occasions when you can persuade others to take action:

- The dinner table.

- Friends and acquaintances who express similar interests.

- At the office during breaks or lunch (as long as it does not interfere with anyone's job).

- Speaking to local groups (everything from churches, to sports clubs, to mother's groups).

- Community celebrations, events, or festivals.

- Town hall meetings. If you are planning to testify in a local public hearing, bring interested friends and family members along to give you support (see Action 17). Their presence will help boost the numbers in your favor and help you feel supported, and they just might become inspired by your activism to become more involved themselves.

One-Hour Rule

There is no easy shortcut here. The best way to recruit advocates is one person at a time through personal contact with the most obvious supporters. Mobilizing a few sophisticated advocates from your district can have a lasting and profound effect on your lawmakers.

Advice from the Field

William C. Miller Jr.

Vice President, Public Affairs

U.S. Chamber of Commerce

"Getting like-minded people to participate on Election Day is the best net to catch the most people for future grassroots activities. Helping people to register to vote, get an absentee ballot, and get to the polls can be a great recruitment tool that can lead to their involvement with actual legislation that needs their support."

PART 3

Get Involved with Elections

Get Out the Vote

In this chapter, you will learn:

- Why you must vote in every election
- Easy ways you can effectively double, triple, or quadruple the power of your individual vote
- Why you might want to register with a political party
- Where you can find out who is running on your local ballot and what their positions on the issues you care about are

"How important is my vote?" It is an honest question in a complicated world where obligations seem to press in from every quarter. After all, unlike most of the other tools outlined in this book, your vote as a citizen of the United States carries the least amount of personal information of any other method of communication with your lawmakers. In a country where everyone is encouraged to share their opinions—in local newspapers, on talk radio, in chatrooms on the World Wide Web—in a country where everyone is constantly talking on their cell phone, a vote might not seem like the sexiest form of self-expression available. And you probably suspect that one individual vote may not ultimately decide any individual election.

Despite its limitations, your vote on Election Day is what establishes the power of all of the other actions described in this book. You very much want to be one of the dwindling number of Americans who can be depended on to go to the polls on Election Day. As our country becomes more cynical or pessimistic about politics, being one of the voters is, more and more, a powerful attribute.

The more you learn about an issue and the more you interact with your lawmakers, the less burdensome voting becomes. Voters who do not engage in grassroots advocacy between elections must rely on nasty campaign commercials to differentiate between candidates. Advocates, however, have a stronger footing on Election Day. Anyone can make a promise to woo voters, but you will know exactly how supportive a candidate has been while in office and the legislative approach that he or she favors on the issues you care about.

Beyond the issues, you might also be able to comment with your vote on how accessible the lawmaker's office is to your letters and phone calls and how competent and accessible the staff he has hired are to constituents.

Whatever factors end up influencing your voting selection, as an advocate, you are at a tremendous advantage over your fellow-citizens who have no real idea if the incumbent has been effective and trustworthy or if the challenger is providing any viable alternatives.

WHY VOTING IS NOT AS EASY AS IT SEEMS

In order to be a voter, you must first register to vote. The United States, world cheerleader for democracy, has one of the least impressive voter turnout records among world democracies. Frequently cited as a barrier to participation is the fact that Americans must register before they vote. By the time you realize that there is a strange and dangerous candidate running for local office, it

One-Hour Rule

If you are not yet registered to vote, do it now. Right now.

Advice from the Field

Ryan Clary

Senior Policy Advocate

Project Inform

"Nothing beats the power and effectiveness of constituents talking to their own elected officials—particularly for those constituents who get to know their representatives during the campaign. They always seem to remember the folks they met on the campaign trail."

might be too late for you to register. To make matters more complicated, voter registration laws are established by each individual state. That means that the deadlines for registration are not uniform across our country.

Several years ago, activists bound together in an attempt to make voter registration easier and more uniform by passing the federal National Voter Registration Act, also known as "Motor Voter." The law, among other things, established a single registration form that would be accepted by all states. The law also provided that departments of motor vehicles and other sites of government services would offer voter registration in addition to the other services they provide. Deadlines for registration still vary from state to state, but at least there is a single registration form can be used no matter where you live.

Advice from the Field

Peter Larson

Director of Development

Metro TeenAIDS

"Don't wait. When I was on the Hill, I noticed that newly elected representatives presented the best opportunity for the grassroots. The best time to make an impact is before this person casts his or her first vote on your issues. At that point, he or she still has a clean record, is learning about the issue, and is trying to gauge what the district thinks about the issue. After a representative has cast a vote on your issue, it is harder to change position because he or she does not want to be seen as waffling."

VOTING IS ACTUALLY HARD WORK

Don't let anyone tell you it isn't. So much time has been spent dumbing down our expectations for American citizens on Election Day that not much attention is given to the amount of research and effort that must truly be expended to cast an intelligent vote. If you are going to be an informed voter, you have to commit to several dates, duties, and deadlines. The sooner you recognize these actions, the sooner you can schedule your time to accomplish them.

Things You Must Do to Be an Intelligent Voter

1. Register to vote by the deadline (or if you have recently moved).

2. Find out who is running in the primary election (at every level of government).

3. Research the candidates in the primary election.

4. Vote in the primary election.

5. Find out who is running in the general election (at every level of government).

6. Research the candidates in the general election.

7. Research any ballot initiatives that you will be voting on in the general election.

8. Vote in the general election.

VOTER TURNOUT AFFECTS YOU

Grassroots strategy requires that you never fail to inform your elected officials that you live in their district and that you always make it to the polls.

Low turnout tells your elected officials that they do not have to be overly concerned with the wants and needs of the district.

Another problem when people don't vote is that extremists can sometimes get elected. Highly mobilized ideological extremists can exert a disproportionate impact on the outcomes of local elections. When an extremist is given public office, we all suffer, but at the same time, we are all responsible.

Just as low turnout can work against you, it can also work for you as long as you are one of the few who actually vote. Low turnout creates the opportunity for your vote to speak louder than it might otherwise. If your neighbors cannot be induced to go to the polls, your elected officials will have that much more time to spend on your concerns and attending to your other requests.

SHOULD YOU REGISTER WITH A POLITICAL PARTY OR BE A POLITICAL FREE AGENT?

When you register to vote, you will often be asked if you wish to register as a member of a political party. If you are familiar with, already support, and want to be identified as such a member, then you should feel free to register with that party.

Many Americans simply throw their vote behind the candidate from their political party when they vote. This is one time-saving strategy you might want to consider. Your political party should have crafted a party platform in line with your general sentiments, and it should have identified and funded like-minded candidates for every level of government in your local elections. In this way, a political party can provide a sort of seal of approval for your vote. But keep in mind that ultimately the party platform is a suggestion, and a candidate, once elected, may choose to uphold all, none, or only part of the platform. Candidates come in many stripes, even candidates from the same political party. There are tax-cutting Republicans, socially conservative Republicans, libertarian Republicans, probusiness Republicans, and moderate Republicans, and Democrats exhibit a similar spectrum of types. You may prefer one kind of Republican or Democrat to another kind.

Strategic considerations of this choice relate mostly to the primary elections. Many states have closed primary elections. In a closed primary, only those who are registered for a particular party can vote for a candidate in that particular party. (In an open primary, anyone registered to vote can vote. So you can vote for the Republican candidate you like best even if you are a registered Democrat and plan to vote that way in the general election.) If your state has a closed primary, you must register with a party, or you will not be able to participate in the primary election and not help determine who ultimately will be on the ballot for the general election.

Another advantage (or perhaps disadvantage) of registering with a political party is that your name and address will be made available to party mailing lists and candidates. This means that you will receive lots of campaign literature about your party's candidates, campaign volunteers will ask if you need help getting to the polls on Election Day, and you might even find a candidate or two knocking on your door to deliver their pitch in person. But if you are annoyed by campaign phone calls and people asking how you plan on voting, you might decide to keep your contact information confidential by not registering with a political party.

Increasingly, with the amount of political information available on the Internet and the power that independents wield in national elections, Americans have chosen to become political free agents. That is, they do not feel especially beholden to a particular political party when they vote. These Americans evaluate the candidates as individuals and might vote for candidates without respect to party affiliation rather than voting the party line every time.

If you want to be independent, that is, a political free agent, you will not be able to vote in the primary election if it is closed.

Whatever route you take, as an intelligent voter, you must do some research on the candidates running for your federal, state, and local offices. Of course, your mailbox may be stuffed with campaign literature before an election, and you will no doubt see some campaign advertisements on television. If your local newspaper is doing its job, even candidates for city council will be profiled and covered, giving you some substance to work with in addition to heavily biased campaign literature and advertising. In addition to these sources of information, you may want to add some sleuthing of your own on-line.

Perhaps the most important piece of information to consider before Election Day is the voting record of the incumbent. All candidates make wonderful promises on the campaign trail, but it is another thing entirely for them to deliver once in office. A voting record helps you reward or punish the actions of an incumbent in office.

If you join an interest group, they might send you a voting report card before an upcoming election that will let you know how your current representative voted on the specific bills related to the issues you care about. If you find that the person who holds office does not vote your way on most of these issues, you may want to throw this person overboard in favor of a fresh politician, no matter what the party is.

GET OUT THE VOTE

Only about half of all eligible Americans cast a vote on Election Day. People don't make it to the voting booth for all sorts of reasons. One of them is that they feel their vote is not likely to affect the overall outcome of the election; there is dry cleaning to be picked up, kids to get to soccer practice, and they haven't even read the paper yet.

Again, it is a central tenet of effective advocacy that you are an active voter no matter what other needs are competing for your attention on Election Day. There are ways that you can boost your influence on Election Day and ways that you can make your participation more significant.

The easiest way to increase the power of your individual vote is to make sure like-minded individuals don't give in to the pressures that are competing for their attention on Election Day. This is especially the case for more sparsely attended elections such as primaries and midterm elections.

Take a person with you to the polls, and you double your power. Get two other like-minded people to the polls who would not otherwise have gone, and you triple the power of your vote. Filling your car with other like-minded voters can quadruple it. And here is the best part: it does not involve proselytizing your crotchety neighbors, your intractable uncle, or your stubborn spouse. You can probably fill your car with friends, maybe even your spouse—people who would vote as you do , but don't vote because they just don't see the point. These people might also be members of a community group to which you belong, like your church or a club, or even the local assisted living facility. All it takes for you to multiply your vote is to provide some additional value to the voting process to these folks who would otherwise not get out to the polls.

The only thing you have to keep in mind is that you cannot take anyone hostage. You are not allowed to go into an election booth with your friends to pull the lever for them. And, please, no ugly scenes where you say, "I drove you because I thought you were going to vote for Jones!" Your friends and neighbors must ultimately vote for themselves without coercion or bribery from you. However, you can certainly discuss the issues, share campaign literature, and most important, make getting to the polls a more exciting experience than it generally is.

You might want to have those little discussions before Election Day, so you can feel out positions on the candidates before you escort your neighbors to the polls. If you discover a friend or family member is supporting another candidate, use your grassroots skills to provide a personal explanation about why you do not feel their candidate will adequately address the issues you care about. You may just get a convert. If not, do not sweat it, and do not make enemies with people you otherwise get along with.

It should go without saying that while you may want to encourage and even escort like-minded voters to the polls on Election Day, you should do nothing at all to impede those whom you believe will vote differently from you on Election Day.

Here are some simple ways to get others interested in going to the polls with you:

- Offer to have lunch with a friend from your neighborhood after you vote.

- Schedule a jog, or a walk, or a bike ride with your neighbors to the polling place and back.

- Offer to drive an elderly neighbor to the polls who might not otherwise go, and offer to combine voting with a few necessary errands.

- Provide a shuttle to and from the polls at your local group or community center.

- Schedule a late morning at the office in advance, and then go out to breakfast with your spouse to review the candidates, issues, and then vote.

- Offer to take turns babysitting with other parents in the neighborhood so you all can get out and vote.

- If you are requesting an absentee ballot, make sure you tell your friends and neighbors and explain to them, if they are interested, how they too can obtain an absentee ballot.

- For friends who take public transportation to work, offer a carpool ride home on Election Day that stops by your local polling place.

- If you are an arts and crafts type of person, make something or bake something. I think red, white, and blue might be best, but I'll leave the color choice and theme up to you. Share whatever it is you make with your neighbors to remind them about Election Day.

- This takes more than an hour, but you can become a polling place volunteer and tell your friends and neighbors that you look forward to their stopping by on Election Day.

Internet Tip

Try the following sites for voter registration forms on-line: Federal Election Commission, http://www.fec.gov, and Congress.org, http://www.congress.org.

For election information related to polling locations, sample ballots, lists of candidates, and similar other matters, find your registrar of voters or elections on your state Web site.

Also look for on-line information about your candidates, the voting records of incumbents, and issue positions at the Library of Congress State and Local Governments Internet Resource Page: http://www.loc.gov/global/state/stategov.html.

Most candidates create Web sites to post their issue positions and voting records, and to solicit volunteers and campaign contributors. Enter any candidate name into your favorite search engine to search for an individual candidate's Web site.

Contribute Money to Candidates Who Support Your Cause

In this chapter, you will learn:

- How campaign contributions help encourage access to elected officials after the winners have taken office

- Why even modest campaign contributions get noticed by lawmakers

- Ways to link your campaign contributions to the issues you care about

- Three different ways you can give money to support your issues in U.S. elections

- The difference between election-based advocacy and legislative advocacy

- Where to find who else gave money to your local candidates and how much they gave

When was the last time you really got something for free in the United States? Thought so.

Complain about it all you want, but money is the mother's milk of American politics. Maybe this will change one day. Maybe our elected officials will be able to turn their backs on cold hard donations and effectively restrict it once and for all. Until then, it is not getting any cheaper to run for public office.

To many, the reality of campaign financing is a distasteful flaw in our system of government. Acknowledged. Your access to democracy should not be determined by how much money you pay for it. The fact that you choose not to contribute to an election campaign should in no way alter the commitment of your lawmakers at any level of government to listen to you.

Despite the purportedly corrupting influence of money upon our elected officials, some aspects of our system remain arguably functional. You can still write a letter to your elected officials even if you are not a campaign contributor, and you can still expect that letter to have impact. You can even write a letter if you gave money to and voted for the other guy and still expect effective representation. Most important, you can still vote, and that vote ultimately will determine whether an incumbent stays in office.

There are a number of journalists, organizations, and voters who believe that money on some level taints our entire system of government—and would take exception to the suggestion that a system of elections reliant on ever-larger donations is in any way functional. You will have to determine your own comfort level with the current state of campaign finance reform.

HOW DO CAMPAIGN DONATIONS AFFECT THE AMERICAN POLICY PROCESS?

Let's look at the influence of campaign contributions on your average, reasonably honest public official. When people write checks to a campaign, the campaign workers make it their duty to find out who these contributors are, what they care about, and to stay in touch. This is not to say that elected officials ignore constituents who do not donate money to their campaign. Every constituent is a possible vote, and ultimately, the votes are what keep an elected official in office, so no elected official is going to ignore a constituent who might help keep her in office. At the same time, running for public office (and running for reelection) are expensive.

It takes a whole lot—a breathtaking lot—of money to run for office and to stay in office. The Center for Responsive Politics found that the average cost of defeating a single incumbent in 2000 was just over $2 million. Your elected officials have to raise that money, and they need to raise it every couple of years. The best way to do that is to keep the people who give them money happy (legally happy, that is). Candidates and incumbents keep contributors happy mostly by listening carefully to their concerns and their ideas. Even if legislators don't vote the way their contributors want them, they are usually willing to engage in discussion about it.

What contributing to an election campaign secures, then, is access—not necessarily your ability to dictate a vote, but perhaps more than a tally mark on a page when you call or write to express concern about an upcoming vote.

Some voters can live with the idea that candidates need to solicit money to run for public office, but decide they cannot possibly contribute as much money to campaigns as do large political action committees (PACs) that funnel millions of dollars to candidates at all levels of government (Example 13.1 shows a PAC report). *This is a missed opportunity.* One of the reasons PACs were created was so that everyday Americans might be able to pool their campaign contributions and compete with other well-financed entities. In fact, campaign finance laws are structured so that PACs are limited in the amount of money they can give to any one candidate. So even if you are aware that some PACs have millions of dollars to contribute, they are giving only a few thousand dollars to any one individual candidate—and you could encourage access for your side of the story if you hold a few modest local fundraisers. On the state and local level, even smaller campaign donations, sometimes as little as twenty dollars, can get noticed by elected officials, who almost always appreciate any support and encouragement that financial contributions make to a campaign.

MAKE SURE YOU GET NOTICED

Candidates running for office can shake only so many hands and attend only so many fundraisers. For that reason, they spend lots of money on direct mail fundraising firms that send out solicitations. These firms develop

Example 13.1. A PAC Report

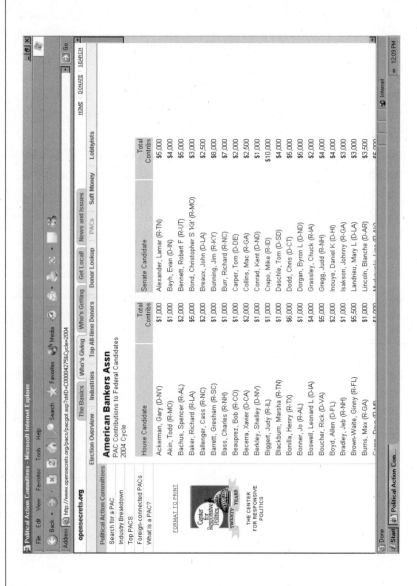

openSecrets.org

Election Overview | Industries | Top All-time Donors | Donor Lookup | PACs | Soft Money | Lobbyists

The Basics | Who's Giving | Who's Getting | Get Local! | News and Issues

HOME DONATE SEARCH

Political Action Committees

Search for a PAC
Industry Breakdown
Top PACS
Foreign-connected PACs
What is a PAC?

FORMAT TO PRINT

THE CENTER FOR RESPONSIVE POLITICS

American Bankers Assn

PAC Contributions to Federal Candidates
2004 Cycle

House Candidate	Total Contribs	Senate Candidate	Total Contribs
Ackerman, Gary (D-NY)	$1,000	Alexander, Lamar (R-TN)	$5,000
Akin, Todd (R-MO)	$1,000	Bayh, Evan (D-IN)	$4,000
Bachus, Spencer (R-AL)	$2,000	Bennett, Robert F (R-UT)	$5,000
Baker, Richard (R-LA)	$5,000	Bond, Christopher S 'Kit' (R-MO)	$3,000
Ballenger, Cass (R-NC)	$2,000	Breaux, John (D-LA)	$2,500
Barrett, Gresham (R-SC)	$1,000	Bunning, Jim (R-KY)	$8,000
Bass, Charles (R-NH)	$1,000	Burr, Richard (R-NC)	$7,000
Beauprez, Bob (R-CO)	$1,000	Carper, Tom (D-DE)	$2,000
Becerra, Xavier (D-CA)	$2,000	Collins, Mac (R-GA)	$2,500
Berkley, Shelley (D-NV)	$1,000	Conrad, Kent (D-ND)	$1,000
Biggert, Judy (R-IL)	$1,000	Crapo, Mike (R-ID)	$10,000
Blackburn, Marsha (R-TN)	$1,000	Daschle, Tom (D-SD)	$4,000
Bonilla, Henry (R-TX)	$6,000	Dodd, Chris (D-CT)	$5,000
Bonner, Jo (R-AL)	$1,000	Dorgan, Byron L (D-ND)	$5,000
Boswell, Leonard L (D-IA)	$4,000	Grassley, Chuck (R-IA)	$2,000
Boucher, Rick (D-VA)	$5,000	Gregg, Judd (R-NH)	$4,000
Boyd, Allen (D-FL)	$2,000	Inouye, Daniel K (D-HI)	$4,000
Bradley, Jeb (R-NH)	$1,000	Isakson, Johnny (R-GA)	$3,000
Brown-Waite, Ginny (R-FL)	$5,500	Landrieu, Mary L (D-LA)	$3,000
Burns, Max (R-GA)	$1,000	Lincoln, Blanche (D-AR)	$3,500

glitzy, emotional mail pieces that seek to entice you to drop a check in the mail with no strings attached. Nothing really makes a local candidate happier than the nameless, faceless check writer (who writes checks as part of direct mail or on-line fundraising solicitations). And there is nothing that is less in your own personal interest.

Two pieces of information are critical for you to signal in any donation you give to an elected official. The first is who you are. Federal election laws prohibit you from anonymously making campaign contributions over fifty dollars as a way to safeguard against fraud, and donations that you make do become a matter of public record. However, you want your elected officials to know who you are by name (and face, if possible). If you create some name recognition as a campaign donor, your future communications might be given special consideration, but they have got to learn your name before that can happen.

One-Hour Rule

Never give a check to a candidate for public office without highlighting your name and signaling the issues you care about.

The second piece of information you want to tie to any campaign donation is the general issue area that you care about. Note that you cannot give campaign donations with requests for specific votes on specific pieces of legislation. That comes too close to outright bribery. What you can do is say that you are a supporter of a general issue area that informs your overall support for that candidate. This is a key difference between communicating in the electoral versus the legislative spheres. When you talk to a candidate, or give money to candidate, or attend a fundraiser for a candidate, you cannot ask the candidate for a specific vote on a specific piece of legislation if that person wins the election. Such discussions can easily be misconstrued as bribery. But when you meet with a lawmaker in the state capitol as an advocate, you are free to urge him to vote a specific way on a specific piece of legislation—but you cannot pull out a campaign check in such surroundings.

If you don't support the good guys, you are making it that much easier for someone who may not care in the slightest about the issues that are important to you to get into office.

TYING YOUR CAMPAIGN DONATIONS TO THE ISSUES YOU CARE ABOUT

There are several ways you can link your name and interests with your campaign contributions:

- Include a written letter with a campaign check noting who you are and the issues you care about and the general position on the issue positions you hope the candidate adopts.

- Alternatively, use the memo line on your check to include a little message, for example, "Haywood for gun control!" or "Hoping for a strong voice on defense."

- Give your check at a small fundraiser or gathering of like-minded people. Rather than arriving in the mail, your check will get bundled with those sent by others who share your concerns and make a collective impression.

- Deliver your check in person to the campaign office (NOT the legislative office) and briefly share your concerns with the campaign manager. Request position papers on the issues you care about. Position papers contain the proposals a candidate supports related to a specific issue area. Requesting a position paper that deals with your issue signals to the office that voters are interested in that issue area.

- Send a separate e-mail or letter to the campaign office explaining that you recently wrote a check and identifying the general issues areas you care about.

You can discuss or make campaign contributions only in a campaign setting (at a fundraiser or in the campaign office). Never offer to write a campaign check when you are in the state capitol or other legislative setting. You must always be careful that you never insinuate that if you give money to a candidate, or if you gave money to a candidate, that you expect a specific vote on a specific piece of legislation. You are allowed to make such requests of your representatives, but they need to be kept completely separate from any discussion about campaign contributions. (Illustration 13.1 delineates the differences between electoral and legislative advocacy.)

Remember, there are very, very few elected officials who would risk the loss of an election, or worse, for one more modest campaign contribution. Any sort of money-for-a-specific-vote rhetoric in connection to your contribution is likely to backfire and make the candidate feel the need to distance herself from both you and quite possibly the issues you care about.

Illustration 13.1. Electoral versus Legislative Advocacy

Electoral Sphere (supporting candidates for public office and any other election-related activities)	**Legislative Sphere** (supporting specific bills and interacting with elected officials in office)
Express support of general issue areas or proposals, for example, "the environment."	Express support of a specific vote on a specific bill, for example, "Vote yes on HR 1234."
Make campaign contributions in a campaign setting.	Never discuss or offer campaign contributions in a legislative office or setting.
Never insinuate that a campaign contribution is given in exchange for a specific vote on a specific bill.	Never say that you expect your lawmaker to give you a specific vote because you were a campaign contributor.
You can say that a legislator's voting record will influence your vote on Election Day.	You can say that a legislator's voting records will influence your vote on Election Day.

OPTIONS FOR CONTRIBUTING

There are three general ways you can financially contribute during election season in the United States, and each choice has its strategic advantages and limitations. You can contribute money to individual candidates, helping you to establish a relationship with an incumbent or future representative. You can donate money to political parties to assist in their overall efforts like party building, polling, and advertising. You can consider giving money to a political action committee where like-minded people pool their financial resources to support candidates who are sympathetic to their views (see Illustration 13.2).

The Congress, in a well-intentioned act of humor, has set limits on each type of donation in an effort to keep the very rich among us from dwarfing the contributions of those of more modest means (see Illustration 3.3). I characterize it as an act of humor because the limits are capped at $95,000 in any two-year period. If that does not seem to quite level the playing field, remember that any individual can contribute only a maximum of

---

Advice from the Field

The Honorable Luis Simmons

Delegate

Maryland State Assembly

"I do notice a $20 check from a regular voter. I appreciate it because the guy is not a corporation and the money means more to him. It counts. It shows you feel emphatically about something."

Illustration 13.2. How Your Contribution Is Used

Type of Donation	Typical Expenditures	Strategic Reason
Individual candidates	• Local advertising • Yard signs • Bumper stickers • Local campaign office • Food for volunteers • Direct mail campaigns	These are the candidates at every level of government that are seeking office to represent you. Financial support from the district is always noticed and appreciated.
Political party	• Statewide and nationwide field of candidates from the same party • Presidential campaign advertising • Organizing activities, such as focus group studies and training of local party organizers • Soft money to help offset operating expenditures, allowing more money to go directly to candidates than would otherwise	Political parties help forge and communicate a unifying platform that can help your local candidates get into office. Parties provide financial and technical assistance to candidates and incumbents and work in general toward gaining a majority at any level of government—essential to successfully implementing a platform that resonates with voters.
Political action committee (PAC)	• Issue advertising • Candidate questionnaires • Key district targeting—especially in terms of protecting incumbents in key offices or attacking those who are consistently contrary • Training for regional coordinators to help local organizers from all over the state or country fight for your issues	Bundles money for candidates from people who care about a specific issue. Works to identify and educate candidates specifically about that issue. Often candidates are educated and then interviewed so that campaign donations are given with clarity about the PAC's position on their issue.

Illustration 13.3. Individual Contribution Limits for Federal Candidates, PACs, and Parties

	To Each Federal Candidate (per Election)	To National Party Committee	To Any Political Action Committee	Total Biennial Limit
Individual	$2,000 per election to any one candidate per election ($4,000 if you contribute to a primary and a general election)	$25,000 in any calendar year. (There is a $10,000 limit per calendar year to a state or local party committee.)	$5,000 in any calendar year	$95,000 in any two-year period (consult the Federal Election Commission for maximum contributions within this limit to candidates versus committees) (Any contributions exceeding $100 must be made by check, money order, or other written instrument—they cannot be anonymous.)

Note: See Federal Election Commission Guide for Citizens at http://www.fec.gov/citizen-guide.html for more detailed information about campaign contribution limits.

$2,000 per election to any federal candidate and any PAC can contribute only $5,000. These may be significant sums to you, but they do give you the chance to compete with the most well-funded interests if you commit to making a few contributions.

When you make financial contributions directly to candidates for public office, you should probably focus on candidates who would represent the district where you live. You can choose to give money to a candidate who represents a different geographical area, but there is no guarantee, on taking office, that your access to that candidate will have certain impact. Geography remains the prime consideration of any elected official, and you cannot simply go out and purchase yourself the lawmaker of your choice. Nevertheless, if you contribute to a PAC, your contribution might very well be used to support candidates from districts all over the state or the nation. PACs usually make a number of donations and work to secure a broad base of support at any level of government.

Internet Tip

You can research the individuals and groups that are making campaign donations to your local candidates. Check out the following sites for more information: Center for Responsive Politics, http://www.opensecrets.org, and Federal Election Commission: http://www.fec.gov.

For information on candidates, issues positions, and more, check out http://www.vote-smart.org.

PART 4

Work the News Media

Start a Press Clippings File

In this chapter, you will learn:

- Easy ways to collect news, statistics, and arguments related to the issues you care about

- How the news media help to identify your opposition and reveal their most powerful arguments

- The easiest way to search the news media for recent articles on the issues you care about

It is often said in politics that information is power. You would be surprised just how much power you recycle over the course of a year if you don't come up with an easy way to save the comments, stories, editorials, statistics, and other immensely valuable pieces of information related to the issues you care about that get presented in the news media.

Start by taking a manila folder, write "clippings" on it, and you are almost done. Keep it in a convenient place, and any time you read something interesting, or historic, or (and these are the best things to clip) just plain eloquent about your issues, rip it out and stick it in the folder. Make sure you keep the source and date on any clipping so you can refer to it later.

Your typical Fortune 500 executive, your typical interest group executive, and your typical political party operative will all regularly employ clipping services so that they do not miss any articles related to their businesses, issues, or candidates that appear in the news media, including the *Washington Post*, the *New York Times*, the *Wall Street Journal*, *Time*, *Newsweek*, and any industry-specific publications. If something is being said about them in the news media, they want to know about it. It is helpful for you to have the same awareness of any news media notices related to your issues, but you will probably have to collect them yourself.

The amount of effort you put into it is up to you. You may wish to subscribe to a wide array of magazines and newspapers to stay on top of the issues you care about. Alternatively, you may just want to keep the mentions that you come across with your morning coffee while perusing the hometown newspaper. Just be ready to rip and file at a moment's notice. You never know when you will read something really great that you may want to save for future reference.

Focus on news media outlets that are credible and serious. You may find some outrageous quotes or statistics

One-Hour Rule

You do not have to save every single mention of an issue found in the print news media, only things that are extremely well written, new, or important.

in a supermarket tabloid, but quoting such dubious sources will tend to detract from your arguments rather than contribute to them. Carefully consider the veracity of any information you find on the Internet.

There are a number of advantages of keeping a clippings file:

• A clippings file forms an informal time line of the politics surrounding a bill. The news media report on historic shifts related to ongoing issues. If the news media are doing their job, they will report when some new piece of information, a study, or an event occurs that changes the nature of the issue that you care about or alters your understanding of it. Novel solutions might be reported as they are proposed. New pieces of legislation might get noticed.

• Sometimes you find flashes of brilliance or undeniable eloquence in clippings. Someone might lay out an argument in a compelling fashion, through sheer argumentative brilliance, that you will always want to remember. Columnists build their reputations around being opinionated and well spoken. Columnists often have license to be more cutting, more humorous, and more opinionated than unbiased journalists can be. You might want to keep their words on file so you know how to present your arguments in ways that are sure to grab other people's attention and make an indelible impression. Pithy quotes related to the issues you care about also can be found in letters to the editor, opinion editorials, human interest stories, and even paid political advertising.

• Articles sometimes provide a gauge of community sentiment. The news media often incorporate polls that indicate if you are winning or losing on an issue and if your base of support is slipping or becoming stronger. Some issues slowly build support over time after years of discussion.

• A clippings file can be used to educate others. When you convince somebody new to take action on an issue, that person will often need some background information. A potential advocate who agrees that your issues are important may have no idea about current legislation or the arguments that historically underpin that legislation. A clippings file can serve as an impromptu training manual for the issues you care about.

• A clippings file is a good place to amass background statistics. Newspapers and magazines often summarize current statistics (for example, the number of deaths related to a given disease or the number of jobs generated by a burgeoning new sector of the economy) and may even present them as nifty charts and graphs. The more active you become in public affairs, the more you will want to pepper your communications with a telling and accurate statistic (not to replace your personal story but to supplement it). Keep your eyes open for compelling statistics or graphics that

Advice from the Field

Dana Kozlov

Reporter

WBBM-TV (CBS affiliate, Chicago)

"If you are fortunate enough to get interviewed in a local news piece, take it upon yourself to buy copies of the newspaper or to tape the show. In bigger markets, we usually don't have the time to pull file tape of past broadcasts and copy them for the people we interviewed because we get dozens of requests each week."

---

you can use to bolster your position. If you pull statistics from the news media, make sure you cite the source of your statistics. Any statistics you collect should not obscure the power of your personal story. Remember that lawmakers are often more interested in local arguments than impressive statistics.

• A clippings file is a good place to keep tabs on the opposition. If you pay attention, you can usually get a good sense of the organizations, the elected officials, and the pundits that are not friendly on your issues. Just as strong arguments in favor of your issue positions should be clipped, so too should any effective arguments made by the opposition. (See Action 7 for more on preparing for the opposition.)

Internet Tip

Sites that allow you to search through many media outlets at one time make it easy for you to scan for any significant articles or reports related to the issues you care about. Try these: NewsLink: http://newslink.org, The Drudge Report: http://www.drudgereport.com, and Total News: http://www.totalnews.com.

Write a Letter to the Editor

In this chapter, you will learn:

- What editors look for and like to publish from their readers
- How letters to the editor and editorials can complement your legislative efforts
- The difference between a letter to the editor and an opinion editorial
- Why being concise with the news media is more desirable than being comprehensive

There is something thrilling about seeing your name in print. Getting your local newspaper to print a letter that you have written seems to confirm that your viewpoint is well reasoned and that you are deserving of serious consideration. But does a letter to the editor or an editorial exert any discernable pressure on the fate of a given piece of legislation?

The news media are not only the best way for you to stay informed about the actions of your government; they are often a primary resource that elected officials use to take stock of their district. In the same way that personal communications with your representatives can help move your issues onto their radar screen, the news media provide another powerful signal to lawmakers on what issues voters care about and the kinds of policies that the district finds palatable.

Accordingly, elected officials tend to be voracious consumers of their local news media, and there is good reason to hope that a letter from you to the local newspaper about a current legislative issue will be clipped by the legislator or the legislative staff and considered. This is not to say that once the local newspaper agrees to publish your letter, your desired vote on a given bill is a sure thing. The news media are at best an indirect way for you to communicate with the decision makers you would like to influence. Letters and editorials in your local newspaper can be powerful, but they complement other, more direct actions and should not replace those forms of communication with your representatives.

Still, editorials and letters to the editor have the distinct advantage of communicating your opinions to other interested voters in your community. A well-written letter in the paper can contribute to a favorable atmosphere

Advice from the Field

Jo-Ann Armao

Assistant Managing Editor, Metropolitan News

Washington Post

"The question I am perhaps asked the most is, What is it we are interested in? What will guarantee press coverage? I don't have a pat, easy formula. Sometimes our interests flow from a current event or national themes, or it's a slow news day and we need stories. Sometimes a story is a story because of the particular interests of a reporter or an editor. That said, here is a good rule of thumb for what generally attracts our interest: something novel, different, unexpected, contrarian."

in the district related to the issues you care about, and this atmosphere will help comfort your representatives when they prepare to vote your way. Although chances are good that your comments on a current policy will be noticed in a legislative office, keep in mind there is no guarantee.

PREPARING YOUR SUBMISSION

Guidelines for submission, including such details as the names and addresses of the editors where you should send your correspondence to and the maximum length of any written submission, are generally printed in your local newspaper on the same page as the letters and editorials. Increasingly, submission guidelines are available on a newspaper's Web site.

Do not agonize over margins and fonts. Your consideration is better applied to the substance of your letter or editorial. As in any other grassroots action, you want to humanize your position by providing some anecdotal examples of how a particular issue affects you or other persons in the district. If you choose a more academic approach—especially if your professional experience allows you to use compelling statistics or to speak more broadly than the anecdote—remember to focus on a critical argument or two and keep the arguments local. Your argument should not read like a dissertation; it should read like a distillation of the most salient points.

Finally, resist any temptation to use your letter or your editorial to punish your opposition through name calling or nasty monologues. It is better—although it probably does not feel better—to use your column inches

One-Hour Rule

If you get published, congratulations! You are an opinion leader! Keep a clean set of photocopies. You can share them during in-person meetings with your lawmaker to signal that you are a visible and vocal member of the community.

to compel support through a sense of fairness and confident concern. Nasty dispatches can sometimes turn people against your issues who might have otherwise agreed with your arguments if only you had presented them in a more gracious fashion.

THE DIFFERENCE BETWEEN A LETTER TO THE EDITOR AND AN OPINION EDITORIAL

A letter to the editor is just that: a letter written to a publication, usually in response to a previously published article. Letters to the editor tend to be brief; a few paragraphs is usually the maximum. They are likely to be edited down to their bare minimum, so if you don't want to take a chance on the newspaper's distorting your sentiments, keep your letters to the editor to a few sentences.

An editorial tends to be a longer piece that argues or educates on some current issue. It does not have to comment on a previously published article, and it tends to be more formal in tone. Editorials are usually written by "experts," that is, people with extensive insight into the issue or with firsthand experience. This is unlike letters to the editor, which can consist purely of opinion and do not necessarily rely on the writer's professional background for credibility.

Opinion editorials tend to be more difficult to get published because newspapers like to reserve this space for experts who are particularly well versed in the issues they cover. Do not let this deter you. Check out the opinion editorials in your local newspaper to get a sense of who they publish and on what topics. You might just be such an expert, and they will welcome a submission from you for their consideration.

THINGS TO KEEP IN MIND WHEN WRITING A LETTER TO THE EDITOR OR AN OPINION EDITORIAL

Remember that your individual story or expertise is your chief consideration when you compose a letter to your local newspaper. Do your best to adhere to publishing guidelines and then focus on the substance of your letter. Here are some guidelines:

Advice from the Field

Bob Ensinger

Director of Communication

Paralyzed Veterans of America

"We encourage our advocates to monitor the news in case something comes up that is related to our issues. Our folks have got to be ready to jump on a news issue that is related to our members when it is hot. We tell them that when the news covers a story related to our issues, they will be looking for a local angle to share. Why couldn't it be you?"

- Familiarize yourself with the newspaper that you would like to submit to. Read the letters to the editor that get published and read the Opinion Editorials—even if they have nothing to do with the issues you care about. These will provide useful insights as to the length of submissions, tone, and people your local newspaper is interested in publishing.
- Include all of your pertinent contact information such as your name, address, phone number, and e-mail address on any submission (preferably with your name on each page). The news media work quickly and may need to contact you if they want to publish your piece.
- Be as rational as possible. Outrageous accusations or cheap shots are not likely to be published. Do not lie or use any statistics that you cannot cite from a credible source. You will be vulnerable to rebuttals from knowledgeable readers who know you are being dishonest.

• Keep it short, and be prepared for editors to make it even shorter. Newspapers will likely edit what you submit, not to alter your opinion on the issues but to conform to available space and their rhetorical style. It is not unreasonable for a letter to the editor to consist of three or four sentences. Word limits for editorials are usually available on-line or by request.

• Do not feel the need to elaborate on every argument you can think of as it relates to a previous article or issue in the news. This will help frame the issue for the readers and lawmakers by implicitly stating that you have isolated the core considerations related to a given issue. Highlight the one or two arguments you believe are most critical for readers to consider. Compelling is better than comprehensive.

• Freely note your credentials. Make sure you identify your expertise, whether you have firsthand experience with the issue in question, or if you have an advanced degree. These things signal to the editor that you are a credible source of information and deserve careful consideration. If your letter or editorial is published, these credentials will signal the same thing to the reader (and your reader might very well be your representative).

• Write when the issue is hot. Don't spend days formulating the most beautifully written letter of your life. The media work quickly, and they are fickle. You may have one day to respond to an article or to send in an editorial before their attention moves on to something else.

• Never berate your elected officials in the local newspaper unless you are certain that you will never request another thing from them as long as they are in office. You can politely urge the action of lawmakers in your letters and even politely express disappointment in a highly professional, impersonal tone. Be extremely careful of ascribing motives to your elected officials that you are not extremely certain of (for example, that your elected official voted against your position for campaign contributions). As much as you might want to humiliate an unhelpful legislator in the local newspaper, you will only harden this person's position by attacking him in print.

• Do not write a letter to the editor every single day on every single issue you can think of. Sending too many submissions may get you noticed—but noticed in a negative way as someone without a clear sense about what the priorities of the community should be.

• Consider submitting your piece via e-mail if the newspaper and magazine allows you to do so. An advantage of on-line submission is that if the media outlet chooses to use your submission, it does not have to retype it. Most newspaper outlets accept submissions by mail or fax as well. Be sure to look in your local newspaper for submission guidelines.

Internet Tip

Try searching these Web sites for listings in your state to find the Web sites, submission guidelines, and word counts for submissions to your local newspapers: NewsLink: newslink.org and NewsDirectory: newsdirectory.com.

PART 5

Super-Powerful Actions That Take a Little More Time

Have a Face-to-Face Meeting with Your Representative

In this chapter, you will learn:

- Why meeting in person with your elected officials is more powerful than even a well-written letter
- How to stay on message in a legislative meeting
- The strategic difference between Lobby Days, fly-ins, site visits, and town hall meetings
- Hook, line, and sinker: the three parts of a legislative meeting
- Common mistakes to avoid when meeting with your lawmakers
- Why to send a thank-you note after your meeting

It is very common for Americans to be nervous when they consider actually meeting with their elected representatives, almost as if our representatives were . . . well, royalty. I thought we had put that all behind us.

Now you do have to be on your best behavior, and it helps your cause immensely if you treat a meeting with your elected officials like any formal business meeting that you may have. But you do yourself and the issues you care about a terrible disservice if you are so intimidated at the prospect of an in-person exchange with your representatives that you regard it as beyond consideration.

Every successive wave of new communications technology has been heralded by grassroots activists as a minimum-effort surrogate for the grassroots organizing of real people. Fax machines, phone banks, the Internet—all have failed to take real people out of the process. There remains no substitute for an in-person exchange between constituents and the elected officials who represent them. An in-person meeting offers the opportunity to infuse your issues with an undeniable sincerity and an almost palpable urgency. You do this just by being there. It is something that technology, so good at communicating, is not able to communicate.

Another reason that in-person meetings with your elected officials are so powerful is that they provide for a dialogue with your lawmakers rather than having you simply tell them how you would like them to vote. Your representative can share how she feels about the issue—why she might or might not support it—in a face-to-face meeting, and you can immediately thank her for her leadership or politely rebut her arguments. In either case, these kinds of dynamic

One-Hour Rule
Meeting in person with your elected officials is the single most powerful grassroots action you can take to fight for the issues you care about.

exchanges can occur only in face-to-face meetings. Beyond the vote in question, this information can help you frame future conversations on the issues you care about.

Perhaps the most powerful aspect of in-person meetings with your elected officials is that they can establish a relationship between you and the people who represent you that can serve as a foundation for future communications—letter writing, phone calls, and e-mail—and permanently

The One-Hour Activist

get you off the tally sheet and into the high-impact realm of truly effective grassroots actions.

DON'T FORGET THE BASICS

When you meet with your elected officials in a face-to-face setting, you have a choice between two approaches to your issue: you can either give a formal argument, or you can relate a personal story from your life, family, or work that helps put your issues and requests into a human, local context.

If you do go the formal argument route, remember to share the one or two arguments (or rebuttals to the opposition's arguments) that you believe are the strongest. Your elected official will probably not have the time or interest to discuss every single argument and rebuttal related to a particular issue. Most legislators do not need much more convincing than your home address. Keep your arguments to a minimum, and clearly tell your legislator the specific action you would like her to take.

If you tell a personal story, you have a good shot at securing a gut-level commitment to your request on behalf of your lawmaker. Like other grassroots exchanges, meeting in-person with your elected officials tends to be brief (usually about fifteen minutes), so you will have to keep your story concise and focused on the details that relate to your request. (See Action 2 for examples of effective personal stories.)

This brings us to your request, sometimes called the ask, in a face-to-face legislative meeting. As with every other grassroots action in this book, you must stay on message if you are working as part of a larger effort. (Illustration 16.1 provides guidance about staying on message.) That means you should not waste valuable time by musing about the stability of your stock portfolio if you are advocating for health research. You can't talk about the hassles of airport security on your trip to Washington, D.C., if you are advocating for the environment. Legislative meetings are short, and if you get distracted from your request, there will not be a clear request for your legislator to act on.

Illustration 16.1. Staying on Message

Why is it so important to stay on message?
• Delivering different messages confuses your issue.
• Grassroots advocacy is successful only if you can persuade a large number of legislators to take the same action toward a single goal.
• It is not fair to your colleagues to deliver a message that was not agreed on or to waste their time by undermining your overall effort.
• Unsympathetic legislators will try to sidetrack you by introducing other issues in your conversation.

What does off-message conversation sound like?
• Discussion about any headlines of the day that are not directly related to your issue.
• Discussion about upcoming elections or partisan politics. This is not only a distraction; if you represent a nonprofit organization, it is probably against the rules.
• Discussion about aspects of your issues that the legislator has no jurisdiction over, such as talking to your Congress member about city problems or state politics.

How do you prevent an off-message conversation?
• Don't participate in a legislative meeting if you do not agree with the request. You can make separate appointments with legislative offices to discuss a contrary point of view.
• Arrange a mandatory premeeting. All attendees should gather before the legislative meeting to review the talking points and prepare their remarks. This will minimize any surprises once you are with the legislator.
• Acknowledge any interesting subjects that come along, but then get right back to your agenda. Practice the following line: "That is an interesting topic, Senator, but we're here today to talk about a different issue." Use this line whenever a legislator or advocate begins to wander.

Example of a lawmaker going off-message
You: That is why cancer research is making a difference in my life, and why we are asking for increased funding.
Lawmaker: I hear that prostitution is really out of control in Bangkok, that very young girls are being forced into that way of life. Talk about a public health problem!
You: That does sound horrible, and I just want to let you know that I came in today to talk about a huge health problem that we have here at home. Now I know we have just a few minutes, so I want to touch on why my request today really helps your constituents who are fighting cancer, as I am.

Example of fellow advocate going off-message:
You: And I just want to underscore that the story I just told you is not unique. The seniors you represent, like me, do need a better way to get our prescriptions that does not consume all of the money we have to live on.
Fellow advocate: Yeah, I heard that Congress might pass a stamp that honors actors and musicians who are seniors. I think that would be great. I would really like to see one for . . .
You: Oh, that does sound great, but I know the Senator has just a few minutes, so maybe you could talk about how much your prescriptions cost and why we came in to support the new Medicare reform bill.
Another advocate: I noticed that you had a lot of interns, and my grandson is coming home from college for the summer. You think he could get a job helping you out with your computers?
You: Let's talk about that after our meeting because we've only got a few minutes, and I think the Senator would really be interested in the story you came to tell about the rising cost of your medicine and how you have had to make some tough choices recently.

Because your meeting will be so short, be careful not to waste any time. Illustration 16.2 sets out common pitfalls for advocates to avoid.

COMMON EVENTS THAT PROVIDE OPPORTUNITIES FOR IN-PERSON MEETINGS

There are several different events that put constituents in face-to-face contact with their elected officials for business-type meetings. Here are descriptions of some of them:

Lobby Day or Fly-Ins

These are the common names for events where interest groups bring people from all over the state to the state capitol or from all over the United States to Capitol Hill for in-person meetings with elected officials that all occur on the same day.

There are several advantages to this. One is that an interest group can demonstrate broad support for a bill by coordinating all of the legislative meetings in the same location and on the same day. Congregating advocates in one place provides groups the opportunity to meet like-minded activists from all over the state or the country. Uniform issue briefing and advocacy training is possible. Most important, perhaps, is the fact that a sizable collection of activists is visible in the state capitol or on Capitol Hill—which lends your issue position some urgency and legitimacy. Finally, meeting in the Capitol allows advocates to discuss their issues in the place where the bills in question are actually introduced, amended, and voted on.

Coordinated Meetings in District Offices

There are advantages to scheduling legislative appointments in the district offices. The main one is that you do not need to fly to Washington and incur the expense of a hotel room to meet with your legislator. District offices are, by their very nature, convenient to where you live. Sometimes access to lawmakers is a little better in the district office because when they are at home, they are not pressed to juggle floor votes and committee work against your

Illustration 16.2. Common Pitfalls to Avoid in Face-to-Face Meetings with Elected Officials

• **Don't go off-message—** Your group's power stems from being able to deliver the same unified message in many legislative offices. Sending a different message is counterproductive and unfair to your fellow advocates.

• **Don't be late or fail to show up at a scheduled meeting—**Punctuality conveys professionalism, confidence, and urgency. (Keep in mind that your legislators might be late to meetings, and remain flexible!)

• **Don't dress down—**Yes, your legislators work for you, but legislatures are formal institutions. Dressing conservatively creates an instant bond with both staff and legislators and invites them to focus on your issue.

• **Don't let them make you too comfortable—**Remember that time is at a premium, and you do not want to waste it searching for chairs or getting coffee.

• **Don't engage in excessive praise or scorn—**You have scheduled a meeting as a credible source of information from the district. Don't distract legislators from that role by being either overly complimentary or verbally abusive.

• **Don't lie or bluff—**If you do not know the answer to a question that your representative asks, you do not need to make up an answer. Tell them you will get back to them with the requested information and then ask your national or statewide group to follow-up with the office. Do not exaggerate your personal stories to make them more dramatic; your lawmakers will be able to sense if something you say is less-than-truthful.

• **Don't argue if they give you a "yes."—**Sometimes legislators will agree with your position for reasons you do not expect. Don't attempt to alter their value system in a brief meeting. Graciously accept their support.

• **Don't discount a meeting with staff—**No matter who you meet with in a legislative office, it is an opportunity to develop a relationship. Staff can be your best ally within the legislative office. Don't treat them dismissively.

• **Don't address unrelated issues—**Addressing a variety of issues makes it difficult for your legislator to guess your priorities and diminishes the importance of your primary issue. Keep the agenda focused.

• **Don't forget to follow-up—**Your meeting never happened if you leave the office, and they never hear from you again. Immediately send a thank-you note, and stay informed on the progress of your issue. Thank the office if the lawmaker votes the way you would like, and request an explanation if he does not deliver on any promises made.

request for a meeting. You might get a little extra time to convince your elected officials to vote your way than you might in the capitol, where so many things vie for your representative's attention.

Unlike a Lobby Day, district meetings are not able to demonstrate a large outpouring of support from across the state or country, but even a small group of constituents from a single district who take time out of their busy days for a meeting with their representative can convince an elected official that an issue should be a priority.

Site Visits

If you take a running start, you can usually slide across the length of the U.S. Capitol on the sheer number of glossy folders that are brought there by interest groups every day. Lobbyists often prepare such folders for any meetings they conduct with an elected official as a way to provide background information and statistics related to their issues. No matter how compelling the statistics inside these folders are, every issue on Capitol Hill tends to look like one of these thin, glossy folders. How can you distinguish your issues in this slippery tide of paper?

A great way to make an issue come alive is to invite your elected officials to come to a business or organization in the district in order to see, feel, hear, and touch the issues that you care about. For example, an advocacy meeting about funding for medical research in the capitol is fine, but it can be extremely powerful to invite the elected official to the local university where exciting research is being done, perhaps talk directly to the scientists, and maybe even see local patients who are being helped by the promise of this new technology.

When the glossy folders arrive in the capitol office, your lawmakers will have an in-depth knowledge of how the issue relates to local constituents if you have provided them with a site visit. Without such an event, your issues can often remain abstract.

Town Hall Meetings

Town hall meetings are a sort of informal gathering between a candidate or elected official and "the People." Usually there is a loose agenda where voters or constituents can line up to ask questions or make statements. The legislator or candidate can address each speaker in turn and promise action, explain votes, or ask for more information. Town hall meetings provide face-to-face meetings with an entire community, usually on a wide range of topics. They are necessarily less focused than office meetings that focus exclusively on one topic, but town hall meetings still provide direct access to your representatives with a minimum of scheduling on your part.

Advice from the Field

Karl Moeller

Government Relations Manager

American Heart Association

"Before inviting a legislator to attend an event, tour a facility, or walk the factory floor, you've got to ask yourself, 'How can we make this event an opportunity for her?' While having a legislator visit is good for you and your group, be sure to point out what the legislator can expect in return when you first invite her. I'm not saying you should throw a fundraiser at the end of the day. Instead, perhaps, you could set up a photo opportunity with school children, give her a podium in front of an assembly line crew at lunch, or provide her a chance to meet three hundred voters from their district whom she wouldn't likely meet otherwise. If you look out for her interests from the start, she'll be more likely to come to your event and want to work with you in the future."

If you get a chance to speak at a town hall meeting, you might be able to make a brief comment or ask a single question. You might get your representative to address your issue briefly before taking the next question.

SCHEDULING A LEGISLATIVE MEETING

Congress members usually have a designated scheduler in the office who handles the many requests for appointments that come in every week. State and local officials may or may not have staff to handle these functions, so you might or might not have to deal with your representatives directly.

A written request is usually required. There is no official format for a written meeting request with a lawmaker, but several pieces of information are usually helpful: who you are (as always, flag that you are a constituent and provide your voting address), the day you would like to meet, what you would like to discuss, and the names and addresses of other constituents who would like to attend the meeting. Be sure to include lots of contact information so that the scheduler can easily get in touch with you. If your legislator agrees to meet with you, there might be several calls back and forth between you and the scheduler to set up a time. Be flexible. Any beleaguered scheduler will find it charming if you are willing to cooperate with their complex schedules.

Often, especially in Washington, D.C., the legislator will not be able to meet with you personally but will instruct a specific staff member to take the meeting, listen to your concerns, and share them at a later time with the elected official. Welcome these meetings, and do not complain about not meeting in person with the lawmaker. Staff have direct access to your elected officials on a daily basis and having them as internal advocates on your issue is invaluable. On many issues, crucial decisions are sometimes delegated to staff. I am not referring to the actual vote, of course, but it is not uncommon for a busy legislator who is not personally invested in a particular issue to turn to the staffer who handles the issue in the office and ask, "How do I feel about this issue?"

HOOK, LINE, AND SINKER: THE THREE PARTS OF A LEGISLATIVE MEETING

Legislative meetings are very brief—usually no more than fifteen minutes or so. That means you do not have a lot of time for idle chitchat. You've got to get right to your issues and your stories, and then make a clear request. Be mindful to reserve enough time to give the lawmaker a chance to respond to your stories and arguments, and most important, your request.

A good legislative meeting can usually be divided into three parts, which I refer to as hook, line, and sinker. Illustration 16.3 provide an example of how this works.

Hook

Hook is who you are. When you sit down to meet with an elected official, the first thing that goes through her mind is the same question that goes through her mind when she opens an e-mail from you or a personal letter: Where do you live? Always, always begin your meeting with a discussion about where you live and work.

Do not generalize about your profession or where you work. If you say, "I work for a major national health care organization," you've just blown your hook. You need to share the name of the street you live on or the name and address of the specific company in the district you work for. A good introduction would be, "I am a radiologist for Shoreline County Hospital on Route 1 in South Wales. I've worked there for seventeen years." Now your legislator is listening because she understands your geography.

Line

Line is your choice: a strong argument or your personal story. Remember that you are going to have to be mindful of the time. As in any other grassroots communication, this is your chance to put a local face on yet another arcane, dry legislative issue. No lobbyist and no low-impact grassroots campaign will have this opportunity. Politely and briefly share what it was that brought you to the issue and why you think your legislator should share your viewpoint. If you don't make it real, nobody else is going to.

Illustration 16.3. Hook, Line, and Sinker: The Three Parts of a Legislative Meeting

Before the Meeting
Arrive ten to fifteen minutes before your appointment and meet with your group. Review your talking points and request, and then review what each person will contribute to the meeting. Assign one person to begin the meeting and one person to end it.

Hook (who you are)
Everyone should briefly introduce themselves at the start of the meeting. This is your chance to remind the legislator that you are constituents. Consider sharing a few unique personal details to underscore the fact that your group represents a broad cross-section from the district.

Line (why you care—local stories and statistics)
Provide the legislator with local stories or a strong argument. Lawmakers especially appreciate real-life examples that put a face on an issue.

Sinker (your request or ask)
Stay on message! Make a clear request of the legislator or the staff. Ask for a commitment, and then listen carefully to the response. Legislative offices often need some time to consider supporting or opposing legislation, but they will often share important insights into their decision-making process. Remember to thank them before you leave.

After the Meeting

Briefly meet with your group outside the office to compare impressions and identify any follow-up work that needs to take place such as sending requested information to the office or reporting the results of your exchange back to the group that scheduled your meeting. Get business cards from any staff you meet with, and send a thank-you note soon after your visit. Such notes help you form long-term, business-like relationships with these offices.

Sinker

Sinker is your request. This is where you have to stay on message if you are participating in a Lobby Day or other organized grassroots event put together by an interest group. If your network is asking for a representative to cosponsor a bill, then you've got to ask her to cosponsor that bill *and nothing else.* Legislative offices are always overwhelmed with their work-loads, so help them focus on a specific action that would help your cause by not piling on extraneous requests.

It is not rude for you to make a specific request of your elected officials. They are often relieved if you give them a single specific action that they can take to demonstrate their support for your issues. You cannot simply ask your lawmakers to empathize with you. Caring is not enough, and they expect you to ask them to take action.

After you have made your request, give your representative time to respond—to share what she thinks about the issue and if she is inclined to see things your way. You do not want to miss out on this feedback by saving your request to the last possible second so that there is no time for the legislator to respond.

WHAT IF YOUR REPRESENTATIVE IS NEGATIVE OR NONCOMMITTAL ABOUT YOUR REQUEST?

Your elected officials will almost always try to make you happy if they can. Sometimes you will be on opposite sides of an issue. If your representative disagrees with your position, do not go into a meltdown. Do not continue to badger him with your reasons. Instead, try to really understand where he is coming from. If you listen to his concerns, he will be more likely to meet with you again in the future, and he will be more open to changing his mind in the future. You, on the other hand, will have the information you need to regroup, perhaps to reframe your arguments to reflect your representative's concerns the next time your communicate.

It is much more common at a face-to-face meeting with your legislator that he will be noncommittal. Lawmakers generally do not like to commit to a course of action until they are able to thoroughly consider the legislative, economic, political, and other impacts of a specific vote. For this reason, they often say that they have to study an issue before making a decision. If this is the case, and it is often the case, thank them for their time, but ask them who you can call in the office to follow-up with so that you will know their ultimate decision and make sure you get a business card from that staffer.

THE THANK-YOU NOTE

Remember to request a business card from any person you meet with in a legislative office so you know where you can send your thank-you letter or e-mail (see Illustration 16.4.).

Illustration 16.4. The Thank-You Note

Sample Note

The Honorable Joe Jones   Sept. 25
U.S. House of Representatives
Washington, DC 20515

I sincerely appreciate the time you took last week to discuss heart and stroke research funding at the National Institutes of Health.

I also would like to thank you for signing our request for increased funding. Such actions mean a lot to constituents like myself.

I am glad we agree that poor Americans must have access to new treatments, even if you cannot support the amount we have requested for research next year.

I hope you have reviewed our sign-on letter and have decided to add your name to this important request, but in either case, please let me know your decision in this matter.

I plan to return to Washington, D.C., next year with an update on how heart and stroke research funding affects our district. I look forward to meeting with you again at that time.

Sincerely,

Lawmaker was . . .
Friendly
Resistant
Noncommittal

Congressional offices are very busy places. An office that can get by being sympathetic during your meeting but without having to take any action once you leave might do so. You must remind your legislators and their staff that you are still watching from home so they follow up on any promised action.

A thank-you note also helps reinforce friendly lawmakers and keeps doors open with those who are less than supportive and underscores your desire to have an ongoing, formal business-like relationship with the legislative office.

Testify at a Public Hearing

In this chapter, you will learn:

- Unexpected things you should expect at a public hearing

- The advantages and limitations of public testimony

- Why to avoid reading a preprinted statement verbatim at a public hearing

- The importance of keeping to your time limit

- How to address your opposition's arguments without creating a conflict in the room

Here is the typical reaction from the devoted advocate, confronted with the prospect of getting to testify at a public hearing about the issues that matter most to him: "You're kidding, right? You're suggesting that I get up in front of a big group of people . . . and speak into a microphone . . . in front of news cameras . . . and my neighbors? . . . Uh, I'm not sure I care that much about world peace."

Public hearings are conducted at every level of government, from the U.S. Congress to your city council, and opportunities are provided for everyday citizens to step up to the podium to deliver a short statement (usually two minutes or less) with the rest of the interested community in attendance. It is a daunting prospect, but one of the first things you notice if you go to a public hearing, as with most other grassroots actions, is that it seems as if the only people talking are your opposition.

Public testimony is one of those classic expressions of American democracy—concerned citizens crammed into high school gymnasiums telling the powers that be that they have had enough. Well, it works in the movies anyway.

Hearings are generally heralded as fine ways for lawmakers to get educated about difficult issues. By holding a hearing, the members of a particular government committee avail themselves of the most outspoken community authorities on any given issue and create a uniform and nonpartisan understanding of the issues before their deliberations begin. Well, not exactly.

In reality, most public hearings are carefully staged, thinly veiled opportunities for political posturing. Often hearings are less a method by which government bodies educate themselves about an important issue under consideration than a way to tout a political party's already-arrived-at position and sell it to the community and the news media.

Parties often divide up testimony slots, carefully pitting one expert against another, and it more resembles a partisan game of chess than a collective search for truth. Invitations to testify are sometimes doled out as favors to important campaign supporters, giving them public exposure.

One-Hour Rule

Never read a written statement at a public hearing if you can help it. Memorize a few key points and speak directly to your lawmakers, making eye contact with legislators who are paying attention to what you are saying.

For these reasons, public hearings are not necessarily the best place to make your initial case about the specific issue you would like to address. In addition to the political posturing, elected officials at public hearings can almost always be seen engaging in side conversations with their staff and colleagues, arriving late, leaving early, and taking frequent breaks, despite the imposition of a more or less courtroom-like decorum on the proceedings.

In an article on the dynamics of the committee system in the *National Journal,* Richard Cohen wrote, "In recent years, the growing number of members seeking to learn about issues often found committee hearings so stage-managed as to be useless, and these members have stopped relying on the committees as a source for education and deliberation. In one alternative approach, small groups of members get together and call experts to their office for private discussions."[*]

SOME WAYS IN WHICH PUBLIC TESTIMONY IS USEFUL

Face-to-face meetings with elected officials and personal letters that arrive well before a hearing date are likely to exert a greater influence on the outcome of a proposed piece of legislation than waiting for a hearing to express your opinion.

This is not to say that public hearings may be safely ignored altogether. Grassroots support of your issues must be demonstrated throughout the entire legislative process, and that often requires some public testimony. If a hearing is scheduled, someone with your point of view had better be willing to speak; a public hearing with no advocates from your side makes a powerful statement for the opposition. Some of the other advantages of public testimony follow:

• Public testimony keeps legislators honest when a vote is taken. Hearings are often followed by voting. In order for you to convince your legislators that your grassroots effort means business, you've got to convince them that you are closely monitoring the bills that you care about. Delivering public testimony lets your representatives know unequivocally that the issue is important to you because you are willing to stand up in a public forum and speak to the issue.

[*]Cohen, R. E. "Crackup of Committees." *National Journal,* July 31, 1999, p. 2215.

• Public testimony provides cover for elected officials who are on your side. Legislators who support risky positions on contentious issues expect to be backed up by groups that agree with them. By providing visible support in a public forum, you are helping to buffer your legislative friends from the attacks of those who disagree with your position, especially if the opposition is mobilized and nasty.

• Public testimony puts a face on the opposition and vets all of their arguments. Attending public hearings is a great way to find out what groups are against your issue positions and to hear the most compelling arguments they have at their disposal. Instead of jeering or grimacing when the opposition testifies, take careful note of who they are, what their concerns are, and how you would counter their strongest arguments.

Advice from the Field

John Goodwin

Grassroots Outreach Coordinator

Humane Society of the United States

"While you may be expected to submit a written version of your statement, it is best not to read your statement when giving it verbally. Instead, speak from memory, and speak from the heart. Even if a legislator asks a tough question, stay calm and dignified. If you do not know an answer, just say so. Don't fudge it, and promise to get back to them with the information they want."

• A big turnout at a public hearing tells the news media that the issue is important to the community. If you have a particularly compelling story, the news media might be interested in granting an interview after hearing your testimony. Even if the local news media do not give you an interview, attending local hearings on the issues you care about can be a constructive way for you to identify the reporters who cover your issues for the news.

WHAT HAPPENS AT A PUBLIC HEARING

A hearing is scheduled by a legislative committee or other group of lawmakers. An agenda is posted in advance of the hearing, usually available by request or on the Internet. Special experts may or may not be invited to testify. (Illustration 17.1 shows the typical setup for a public hearing.)

Typically, public meetings follow a common format:

1. Citizens sign up to speak. Upon their arrival, those who would like to speak must put their names on a list next to the agenda items they wish to address.

2. The hearing is called to order by the committee chair. Usually lawmakers engage in some housekeeping and may make introductory statements before beginning to consider the first item on their agenda. A specific amount of time will generally be allotted to each agenda item for public comment.

3. The chair will notify speakers of a time limit that all must recognize when they make their statement. Individuals' speaking pro and con for a particular agenda item are usually called in alternating fashion, but each legislative body will have its own format for conducting hearings. You may be asked to come to the front of the room and sit at a table next to your opposition. Alternatively, you may be lined up behind a single microphone. Other times, pro and con positions have separate podiums. If you notice lawmakers who are not paying attention, talking to colleagues, or snoozing during the hearing, ignore them and direct your comments to those who seem the most receptive to what you have to say.

Illustration 17.1. Components of a Typical Public Hearing

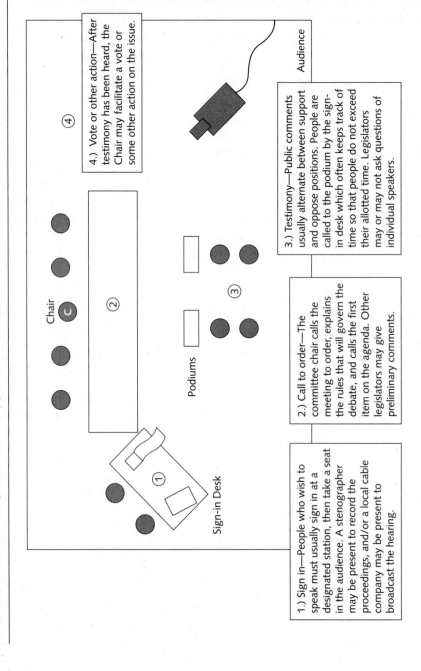

Chair

1.) Sign in—People who wish to speak must usually sign in at a designated station, then take a seat in the audience. A stenographer may be present to record the proceedings, and/or a local cable company may be present to broadcast the hearing.

2.) Call to order—The committee chair calls the meeting to order, explains the rules that will govern the debate, and calls the first item on the agenda. Other legislators may give preliminary comments.

3.) Testimony—Public comments usually alternate between support and oppose positions. People are called to the podium by the sign-in desk which often keeps track of time so that people do not exceed their allotted time. Legislators may or may not ask questions of individual speakers.

4.) Vote or other action—After testimony has been heard, the Chair may facilitate a vote or some other action on the issue.

Sign-in Desk

Podiums

Audience

4. The committee chair ends the testimony on a given item when the list of speakers is exhausted or time runs out. The chair usually thanks everyone for sharing their opinions or arranges to continue the testimony at a later date. Sometimes testimony is followed by deliberation between the elected officials and possibly a vote.

Lawmakers may deviate from their printed agendas or timetables at a public hearing. Remember that they run their hearings and will not tolerate any unsolicited input on their procedures.

Following are some do's and don'ts when attending a public meeting:

Do

- Do watch your local hearings on cable television if they are broadcast as a way to become familiar with the format of your own local hearings. You will notice that many of those who provide testimony are regular community members, just like you.

- Do arrive early. You will usually have to sign up to speak, and generally the sooner you sign up, the sooner you will get to deliver your testimony. Arriving early can also help you get a good seat and get acclimated to the surroundings.

- Do dress professionally. Your personal appearance should convey concern, respect, integrity, and professionalism. The best statement in the world is undercut by slovenly dress that says you don't really care.

- Do be mindful about how you introduce yourself. Give your address if you are the constituent of one of the lawmakers on the dais. The few words you say about yourself at the beginning of your statement also represent a strategic opportunity to establish your professional expertise or personal connection to the issue.

- Do clearly state if you support or oppose the agenda item you are addressing.

- Do be unfailingly polite. As with any other communication with elected officials, seek to build a long-term professional relationship.

- Do succinctly answer any follow-up questions from legislators. This is not a chance for you to redeliver your statement as much as it is an opportunity to show that you are willing to be helpful and that you are confident and professional.

- Do take notes when you are not delivering your statements so you remember what questions different legislators asked, what the arguments of the opposition were, and how each lawmaker voted, if a vote was taken. Sometimes you will be inspired by a story or statistic given by advocates in support of your own position and want to jot it down for future use.

- Do address strong arguments from your opposition as part of your comments. If you can incorporate a rebuttal to an argument that has resonated from the other side, do it. You do not want to turn and face the speaker who made the original argument, and you do not want to be petty or demeaning, but at the same time you do not want the opposition's arguments to stand without a response if you have one. After you tell your personal story, you might say, "That is why I am so confused by what I am hearing from the other side. My story shows that the opposite is true."

Don't

- Don't read from a written statement. It is almost impossible to engage somebody's attention when you are looking down and reading. Memorize a few simple points, and try to speak from memory. More complete statements and supporting materials can usually be submitted to be included in a public record of the proceedings; they do not need to be read in their entirety. Example 17.1 provides notes that a speaker might prepare for giving public testimony. A longer, more formal statement may have been submitted before the hearing, but the speaker opted not to read the statement verbatim.

- Don't exceed your time limit. If the chair informs you that you are out of time, immediately thank the person and sit down. Refusing to stick

Example 17.1. Sample Public Testimony Notes

Notes for public testimony

• Hello. I am Shelby Wilbourne, and I am an ob-gyn physician from Anywhere, Maine.

• I am testifying in support of HR 2345, the tort reform bill.

Point 1: Last March, my liability premiums increased from $33,000 a year to approximately $108,000 despite my spotless record and dedication to my patients' health care.

Point 2: I provided 12 years of practice in the community to more than 8,000 patients. Our local patients really depended on us and trusted us.

Point 3: I had to move practice to another state. Other good doctors from the state are in the same predicament.

Thank you!

(2 minutes maximum! And stay on message!)

He leads with his address to let them know he is a constituent and also signals that he is a doctor, a professional expert on the issue.

Makes request early, including specific bill number and very brief description of the bill.

He uses brief notes to help him stay on message, but does not write out anything to read verbatim.

Unfailingly polite throughout the exchange.

He writes down important presentation tips. He does not want to go over the allotted time for any reason, and he wants to make sure he stays on message.

to time limits makes you look inconsiderate, disorganized, and insecure, and it is not fair to the other side. Simply say, "Thank you."

• Don't chastise the lawmakers for not paying attention. Deliver your statement without interruption no matter what is happening on the dais. Help focus your concentration by making eye contact with those who are listening.

• Don't heckle or bait the opposition. You want to carry the day for your side with your arguments, not how much you can bully the other side. Remember to refrain from making faces when the opposition is speaking, and hush anyone else on your side who is being impolite. Such outbursts appear childish and desperate. You can address faulty arguments professionally and confidently in the body of your comments at a later time.

Internet Tip

Federal committee meetings and hearings can be found at the U.S. Senate and House Web sites: U.S. Senate: http://www.senate.gov, U.S. House: http://www.house.gov, or on THOMAS: http://thomas.loc.gov.

State and local hearing schedules, agendas, and announcements should be posted on the Web. To find them, try the Library of Congress Internet Resource Page of State and Local Governments: http://www.loc.gov/global/state/stategov.html.

Participate in a Protest

In this chapter, you will learn:

- Situations where a protest is strategically appropriate and the times when it is not

- The importance of selecting the right location for a protest

- Why short, memorable slogans are important

- Important precautions to take before and during your participation in a protest

A protest is our birthright as Americans. Nothing makes us feel quite so patriotic as a mild revolution—marching through the street, shouting our demands, justice on our minds. A good demonstration can give us a better feel for democracy than any number of Independence Day parades.

Many people think of protests as the first and only legitimate grassroots action that citizens can engage in, but a protest's limited ability to convey information (usually restricted to a few pithy chants backed up by an angry show of popular support) should make us carefully consider when to use a protest as opposed to more information-rich methods of communication, like directly sharing our stories and concerns in face-to-face meetings with our lawmakers—or sending personalized letters from the district. Americans' ignorance about the legislative process and cynicism with lawmakers in general make them overlook the comparatively easier and more persuasive options of directly making demands of their elected officials.

Still, protests are dramatic, can attract the news media to your issues, and are inspiring to the participants (if not to the people watching at home on television). They have played undeniably fundamental roles in some of our most historic and difficult policy quagmires, such as the battle for civil rights. Such struggles continue to arise in our country and remind us that freedom and justice may never completely be secured, even in the United States, and that they do not survive without attention.

At such junctures, when there is an overriding moral imperative for change, when people in significant numbers are dissatisfied with representation that obstinately refuses to be representative, and when the more collegial confines of legislative offices smack of impotence, then it is time to stage a protest.

One-Hour Rule

Strategically, protests are best employed as a grassroots tool of last resort when more substantive channels of communication have been closed.

If it is done at the right time, by the right people, with the right messages, a protest can alter the course of this nation. Martin Luther King, Jr., remains this country's pioneer organizer of peaceful protests and serves as both instructor and inspiration to those who stage our current and future demonstrations.

The central component of a successful demonstration is some kind of peaceful disruption. A typical protest in the United States is engineered to avoid any serious risk of bloodshed but still disrupt some critical function of the community. The AIDS advocacy group ACT-UP staged a sit-in to stall commuter traffic in New York's Grand Central Station in the 1980s to bring attention to the burgeoning AIDS epidemic, a devastating public health crisis that was being ignored by many in government.

Sometimes disruption can be dangerous and violent, as the deadly Kent State massacre proved in the 1970s. It remains a cautionary tale to anyone who considers participating in a protest. Activists must always keep their eyes and ears open for trouble. Such gatherings, especially when precipitated by anger, can be capricious.

THINGS TO CONSIDER BEFORE PARTICIPATING IN A PROTEST

In some situations, a protest is strategically appropriate, and at other times it is not. Here are some things to consider before participating in a protest:

• Is there a moral imperative at stake? Not every issue—in fact, very few—involves such injustice that people in sufficient numbers will allow a significant disruption in the daily patterns of their lives to alter their opinion about some issue. Without serious moral grounding, the act of upsetting the day-to-day lives of a community ends up being little more than irritating.

• Are other channels of communication closed? Protests are best used as a weapon of last report when more direct, substantive conversations with the powers that be are not possible. Legislators usually welcome interaction with the people they represent and often try to address their needs. Try working within the system before you take to the streets.

• Is the protest well organized? A protest involves a great deal of preparation that must be undertaken by some group of organizers. There are often permits to secure from the local government, press releases to send out, protesters to be recruited, and short messages to be crafted—messages that are easy to remember and fun to yell, messages that bear repeating (for hours). It is now common for large-scale protests to set up safety tents, water stations, and bathroom facilities and to secure legal help should anything go awry—all before the protest begins to roll down the street. There may be civil obedience training before the protest begins where lawyers explain what your rights are and what to do if you get into trouble. Arrive early, get the training, and be sure to ask any questions you might have.

• Will the protest help identify and motivate supporters for your issue? Protests can bring like-minded strangers together and provide a sense of direction and support that can be channeled into future efforts.

• Have you helped organize good attendance? Encourage friends and neighbors who feel the same way that you do to attend. If a lot of people do

Advice from the Field

Pete Sepp

Vice President for Communications

National Taxpayers Union

"We came up with a unique idea for a protest. Instead of assembling a crowd of demonstrators on foot, let them drive to your rally. Pick an auto-accessible landmark on a well-traveled route in your town, such as city hall, and assemble a small number of your members with signs encouraging motorists to honk in support of your cause as they drive by. Publicize the "drive-by" rally in advance with local radio talk show hosts. Citizens who are otherwise too busy to attend a rally on foot will be more inclined to take a five-minute detour on their way to or from work for the chance to make a little noise while remaining in their cars. This type of rally proved particularly effective in Tennessee, where citizen groups organized several 'honk if you hate the income tax' rallies that circled the state capitol building for hours on end."

not show up, the protest will lack the feeling of a compelling outcry from "the People."

• Have you notified any news media contacts you might have? If your elected officials refuse to meet with you, you want the general public to know. Make sure your group sends out a press release with the date, time, and place of the protest. If the news media show up, treat them kindly, and assist them with their stories. It is totally self-defeating to turn your anger on the news media just because they show up to cover your event and share your protest with the broader community. Getting the news media to show up is usually the whole point of a protest.

PERSONAL PREPARATIONS

The sheer size and unpredictability of some protests means that you will have to take care of yourself. A protest is seldom perfectly neat, mannered, or thoroughly pleasant, so make your personal preparations:

• Always, always have a legal form of picture identification whenever you are at a protest.

• You should be in good physical shape; have dependable transportation, and have plenty of food, water, any required medicines, and some cash.

• Inform someone who will not be attending the protest that you might call them if you get into trouble (by getting arrested, for example). Make sure this person is willing to help track you down if he or she doesn't hear from you by a certain time.

• Decide if you are willing to be arrested. Some disruptions spark police interventions. No matter how much sympathy you share with the issue at stake, no one can tell you to get arrested, and no one but you will have to face the consequences if that happens. Common consequences might be long hours in a jail cell, fines, and community service. Your causes might or might not personally justify risking arrest (not for any sort of violent act, mind you, which remains reprehensible no matter what the cause). You must decide for yourself. If you are not willing to be arrested, you will want to remain vigilant during the course of any protest you participate in and decline to participate in any actions that are likely to result in arrests.

• Be mindful of your physical safety. If you are not in top physical shape or do not want to take any chances, you might choose to stay on the fringes of any big group and away from the front lines where the most dramatic clashes are likely to take place. It is important that people who are loud, brave, and colorful spearhead your protest, but these folks are also the first to take any sort of verbal abuse from the community (and hopefully nothing worse than that). No one will likely ask if you want to be a front liner; you must make that determination for yourself.

The point of attracting news media attention and disrupting the community is to change minds and hearts, not to stir up eternal hatred for everything you represent. Signs, T-shirts, loud voices, sincere demonstration of emotion, and all manner of creative high energy are the order here. You want to showcase compelling stories and striking images, and you want to remain articulate despite your anger. You want to be outrageous to a point; you also want to encourage and support others in their outrageousness. Nothing is a bigger drag (to employ a '60s phrase) than a protest participant who spends all of his or her time chastising the other participants for being too loud or too angry. That's the whole idea. At the same time you have to strike a balance. Avoid ridiculously combative, insulting, or un-American sentiments and images, but unless you are willing to hold up signs, or blow whistles, or chant, or march into the street, a protest might not be your calling.

PROTEST DON'TS

Even protests have a list of common don'ts:

• Don't vandalize any property. You will be held liable for any damage that you cause. A protest is not a free pass to destroy property, and any message you have will be overshadowed by any physical damage you leave in your wake.

- Don't be violent. Do not assault anyone or otherwise recklessly endanger anyone's health or well-being. Violence is almost never justified, even when fighting for cherished freedoms.

- Don't be quiet if someone near you flashes a weapon or attempts to stir up violent hatred in the crowd. Notify an official protest organizer or the police of the danger right away. In the same vein, keep an eye out for your fellow protesters. Historically, police have been known to sometimes be overly rough with protesters. The best way to encourage even-handedness from the police is to refrain from violence while sticking together as a group.

- Don't continue protesting if you secure a victory. If an elected official caves in and agrees to meet with your group, you've won! Don't be boorish by refusing to meet with the elected official. If you immediately agree to hold a face-to-face meeting, you can inform the press of any resulting promises or actions right away.

Remember that the ultimate goal of a protest is not to punish, but to open and nurture greater channels of communication with those in power. Any dialogue should be considered a victory, and you and your fellow protesters should savor such achievements.

Volunteer for a Political Campaign

In this chapter, you will learn:

- Why volunteering for a political campaign can provide ongoing access to an elected official
- How to make yourself and your skills useful to the campaign without becoming a nuisance
- Your campaign volunteer bill of rights
- Seven things you should never do in a candidate's campaign office

Volunteering for a local candidate can be time-consuming and might involve such thankless tasks as stuffing envelopes and disturbing your neighbors at dinnertime to ask how they will vote. It can sometimes be grueling work. For all of these reasons, a candidate for public office who relies on you as a campaign volunteer will be indebted to you for life. If elected, she will be sure to read the letters you send to her office and be happy to schedule face-to-face meetings with you and the groups you represent.

Unlike financial contributions, volunteering costs you nothing and has the distinct advantage over a check of giving you face-to-face access with the candidate over a prolonged period of time. If you do volunteer, work hard, for your candidate must win the election in order for your access to pay off.

Your time commitment as a campaign volunteer might necessarily exceed an hour, but it need not become unmanageable. You can usually schedule the days and times of the week that are most convenient for you. You might even decide to restrict your volunteer work to get-out-the-vote efforts on Election Day rather than making a long-term, ongoing commitment.

Take a few moments to consider the kind of work you would most be interested in doing before you offer to volunteer for a local campaign (but remember that the tasks candidates need help with are not always glamorous). Share this information with the volunteer coordinator when you

Advice from the Field
Honorable Richard S. Madaleno Jr.
Delegate, State of Maryland

"One of the most important aspects of any campaign is door knocking. So much of a campaign comes down to voter contact, and if you are not comfortable communicating with strangers, there are not always a lot of other volunteer tasks to offer. On the other hand, door knocking is much easier than people expect. People are usually thrilled that you come to the door because you are generally seeking someone who is interested in the political process. Very rarely do you find someone who is not happy to see you."

initially meet. As a rule, however, there are a lot of mailings, phone calls, and other work that needs to get done, and you must be flexible.

Let the campaign manager (and the candidate when you meet her) know that there is a particular issue area that brought you to the campaign. If you do not state your interest in an area, the candidate will likely assume that you are volunteering because you are an active supporter of the party or because you just like her as a person. Because this is the electoral sphere of politics, you cannot predicate your volunteer work on a specific vote for a specific bill, but you can speak about your issue in general. You can ask for leadership from the candidate, if elected. Once you have shared this information, do not continue to badger the candidate or her staff. One brief conversation is enough for her to get the message unless she asks for your personal insights and ideas related to the issues you care about.

As the election draws closer and the campaign heats up, the campaign manager might ask you to give more time to the campaign. If your time and interest permit, give more. If not, stick to your guns, and do not feel guilty: you have been clear about what you can give from the beginning.

One-Hour Rule
Establish your limits before you volunteer for a local campaign, and stick to them.

YOUR CAMPAIGN VOLUNTEER BILL OF RIGHTS

It is incumbent on you as a volunteer to be professional and flexible. You are there to help the candidate, and the candidate's needs always remain center stage in a campaign office. At the same time, the candidate has some responsibility to treat all volunteers with appreciation and respect. Here are some of your rights as a campaign volunteer:

- You have the right to meet the candidate briefly in person and explain why you have decided to support this bid for office.

- You have the right to have issue positions sufficiently explained to you so that you can accurately represent them as part of the campaign.

- You deserve water, a serviceable bathroom, and even snacks (if there is no place nearby to get food).

- You are allowed to take breaks (although you are there to work hard and professionally).

- You have the right to sufficient training for the tasks you are being asked to perform. That means that you should not be put on the phones without being told who you are calling, what you are saying, and how it fits into the overall campaign strategy.

- You do not have to do anything you are uncomfortable doing or that your health is not suited for.

- You do not have to stay late into the night, especially if you do not feel safe getting to your car or home from the campaign office.

- You do not have to be berated or insulted.

- You do not have to do anything illegal, like vandalizing an opponent's office, property, or mail.

- You have the right for the campaign manager to consider your special skills if they relate to available tasks in the office. If you are a publicist, for example, you might offer to send out press releases if press releases need to be sent out (but you must remain flexible).

If any of these are lacking, quit the campaign and do not return. Consider sending a letter, as professional in tone as possible, directly to the candidate explaining why you chose to discontinue your volunteer work for the campaign.

WHAT YOU DO NOT HAVE THE RIGHT TO DO AS A VOLUNTEER

Just as you have rights, there are seven things that you should never do as a campaign volunteer:

- You do not have the right to use the campaign's phones, computers, and other machines for personal business.

- You are not allowed to bring friends and relatives to hang out in the campaign office while you volunteer.

- You are not allowed to drop by, eat the food, drink the coffee, and then leave without working.

- You are not allowed to monopolize the candidate's time by always insisting on engaging him in conversation, fawning over his every word, or offering your opinion on every issue.

Advice from the Field
Frank Ryan

Manager, Political Education,

ADPAC, American Dental Association

"We try to provide opportunities for our PAC members to become involved in local elections. In the last national election, our dentists invited colleagues to their homes for pizza and beer and to call fellow dentists and their families on behalf of pro-dentistry candidates. By focusing on dental families, volunteers were able to highlight issues of personal importance to voters. Everybody gets calls encouraging support of a candidate. But how often do we get calls from a professional peer, with similar concerns, asking us to support a candidate?"

- You are not allowed to talk to the news media without permission or to assume any other strategic decisions on behalf of the campaign without the blessing of the campaign manager or the candidate. This includes changing a phone script, disseminating alternative issue positions, or spreading rumors about the opposition from the campaign office.

- You may not complain, sow seeds of dissension, or contrive in any other way to dampen the morale of other volunteers, even if you are unhappy. Simply leave the campaign with dignity. If you feel particularly unappreciated or abused, start volunteering for the opponent's campaign.

- Should your candidate win election, you cannot browbeat him to vote your way on a given piece of legislation simply because you volunteered for the campaign. You can expect a face-to-face meeting to share your arguments related to a specific bill and a careful reading of any communications you send, but you cannot force a vote.

Pitch a News Story or Interview

In this chapter, you will learn:

- The kinds of stories that editors and news directors like to put in the paper and on the air
- How to know if a local event is newsworthy
- Why calling a local reporter is more effective than sending out a press release
- Where you can find contact information for your local news media on-line

For the American citizen who wishes to become an active participant in the local news process rather than a passive recipient of the nightly news, the news media can make anyone feel small. The news media's undeniable command of citizen attention, its global reach, its access to information, its command of technology, and its attraction to our political leaders can make the notion of contacting the news media as daunting a prospect as meeting face-to-face with your elected officials.

It may surprise you just how interested, even desperate, the news media are for the local stories and expertise you possess. Like elected officials who welcome local stories and statistics to help illuminate the issues before them, the news media, especially broadcast news media, need your input. Local news media often cannot effectively present a story if they cannot include a local, human aspect of that story. TV news refers to these as "visuals," and they are the lifeblood of a news broadcast. Newspapers rely on visuals to a lesser extent but still use personal stories to make their articles more accessible to readers.

Indeed, most journalists develop a list of sources within the community—people who can provide information on specific issues whom they regularly tap for information or interviews. These sources often include elected officials or knowledgeable experts, but they also are everyday people who can discuss the personal impact an issue has had on the community from the view of a local resident.

For these reasons, you might consider contacting the news media if you have a compelling story about an issue that is currently in the news. (Example 20.1 has a sample script for pitching a news story.)

Unlike your elected officials, who will almost always respond to your requests because you are either a constituent, a campaign contributor or volunteer, there is tremendous competition every day to get the attention of the news media. Reporters do not take every story that is pitched to them by a member of the community. You must be willing to call reporters again even if they do not take all of your story ideas. This work can be poorly suited for those who cannot stand rejection. (If you have not experienced rejection before, you might want to give it a try; it might not hurt nearly as much as you expect, and there may be a budding public relations person inside you ready to pitch your issues to the news media.)

In addition to daily, unrelenting competition for column inches and airtime, the news media focus attention on the most important issues of the day only when something "newsworthy" has happened. Your issue may be of daily, burning import to you personally, but unless something related to the issue dramatically changes, the news media will ignore your issue in favor of the day's more dynamic offerings. Any policy issue is bound to come around periodically, and you must always be ready to contact the news media to offer an interview. As with all other grassroots actions, the more personalized and local your story or arguments are, the more likely a reporter will be to respond to your inquiry. Like other grassroots actions, if

Example 20.1. Sample News Media Pitch Script

Reporter: Hello, WJTV.

Janet: Hello, may I speak with Bob Williams?

Reporter: This is Bob Williams.

Janet: Hello. My name is Janet Ellsworth. I live in Shady Hill, and I am calling because I saw your piece on the news last night about a Constitutional Amendment banning same-sex unions.

Immediately establishes that she is local and not a PR professional.

Reporter: What did you think?

Janet: I thought you did a really good job of showing both sides of the issue. It seems like you had to rely on official spokespeople from both sides, and I wanted to let you know that my partner, Carrie, and I have been in a loving relationship for twelve years right here in Shady Hill.

Is familiar with reporter's work and complimentary even though she clearly thinks he did not capture the whole story.

Reporter: Is that a fact?

Janet: I understand that there are concerns about same-sex unions. At the same time, claims that people like Carrie and I want to undermine American society are really not accurate and not fair. I have talked this over with Carrie, and we have decided that we are willing to be interviewed at home if you are interested.

Is respectful of the opposition. Offers to be interviewed at home thereby providing an interesting visual.

Reporter: Have you talked with any of the other stations?

Janet: You are the first one I called because I saw your story last night.

Gives the reporter the opportunity to have an exclusive, an interview no other station will have.

Reporter: I cannot make any promises, but I would like to pitch this story. We did just cover this issue last night so my news director might not go for it. If we are interested, can you be interviewed today?

Janet: Yes, just let me know a time that would be convenient for you. Carrie and I can meet you at our house which is right near downtown Shady Hill.

She is available to be interviewed at the reporter's convenience that day.

Reporter: Okay, let me get a number where I can reach you, and I will get back to you.

Janet: Thanks so much.

Is unfailingly polite throughout entire exchange.

you establish a relationship with a reporter who cares about your issues, she will be likely to contact you and cover your issues over the long run.

And then there is the issue of balance. Any sort of controversy or hard news angles will send your local reporters to your opposition to solicit their side of things. The news media, at their best, are impartial and balanced, and you must be comfortable with the idea that a reporter you pitch a story to will give equal time to those who oppose your position.

The reporter and the activist often have different goals. The activist wants to create awareness for a given issue in the strongest possible light, with the best possible arguments, and include all important details. A reporter often wants to present the widest range of opinion on a current issue without delving unnecessarily into complex detail. The reporter and her news media outlet control the

One-Hour Rule

If you have a compelling story, don't wait for the news media to find you. Contact them, and offer to be interviewed.

final product. It will not look like a commercial for your issue, but it might include your side of the story.

For the broadcast media (radio and television), you can contact either the assignment desk at the station or any of the on-air reporters you feel have some understanding of or sympathy for the issue in question. The news director and reporters constantly meet to develop story leads and ideas, and any one of them can pitch your story for the next broadcast. For the print media (local newspapers and magazines, for example), you can contact either the editor of the appropriate section of the newspaper or a reporter you respect who has intelligently covered a related issue in the past.

INTERVIEW TIPS

You do not always need to pitch original news stories to get the attention of the news media. If a story related to the issues you care about is currently in the news and you can share local expertise or perspectives, you can call local news media outlets and offer to be interviewed. Here are some tips to keep in mind when pitching your local news media and, if you are lucky, getting interviewed by them.

Contact the News Right Away

The news is a fickle medium. Very few issues make it into the newspaper or onto the news broadcast on a given day. If your story might be news, don't procrastinate. If it turns out that a news outlet cannot use your story or is frankly not interested, don't take it personally. Call again the next time the

Advice from the Field

Dana Kozlov

Reporter

WBBM-TV (CBS affiliate, Chicago)

"If you call a news reporter, and they do not cover your story, do not take it personally. There are no guarantees. Last week, I had set up an interview for a story, but then we had breaking news— a high rise four-alarm fire that we covered live from 5 P.M. to 7 P.M., so needless to say, the story I had planned to do was scrapped. If you keep calling with good story ideas—stories with local hooks or new information—eventually you will break through, and we will cover your story. But we always appreciate ideas."

opportunity presents itself. You just might make it into the newspaper on a different day.

Return News Media Calls Promptly and Keep Yourself Available

The news media work on extremely tight deadlines. The 11:00 P.M. news broadcast comes whether or not the reporters have the perfect interviews or an in-depth understanding of the issues they present. If you agree to be interviewed by the media, you are agreeing to be flexible and available that day and to remain in contact by phone or e-mail.

If You Have an Especially Important Message, Repeat It Frequently During Your Interview

This is a cardinal rule for advertising executives and political activists alike. If you want a particular message to be used as a sound bite, repeat it so that the reporter is not likely to overlook it or underestimate its importance. A reporter may get frustrated if you refuse to answer questions directly in favor of repeating some hallowed sound bite, so use your discretion when you engage in repetition.

Don't Ramble

Most broadcast news stories clock in at under a minute. Newspaper articles are also incredibly compact pieces of information. When you are asked a question, don't ramble on and on. Reporters need sound bites—brief quotes that they can use. Don't get mired in conveying pointless details related to a given issue. Try to encapsulate your story or position in a few snappy sentences. If you are not able to express yourself in a concise manner, a local reporter is not likely to call on you again—not because you don't possess sufficient knowledge about the issue, but because she cannot make use of your meandering comments.

Don't Proselytize

The news is not going to provide a free commercial to air your opinions. Newscasters are interested in your story or your expertise as it relates to a larger news piece that will attempt to be impartial and will necessarily

Advice from the Field

Nancy Weiner

Correspondent, ABC News

"You want to make sure that you speak clearly, emphatically, you want to look directly at the interviewer, and you want to speak in short sentences. If you feel you've delivered a point in a long-winded fashion, ask if you can answer the interviewer's question again. Keep in mind, for television, they will use a sound bite that is no more than a few seconds long."

include other viewpoints. Make your peace with this reality. Respond to the questions they ask and give the information that they are looking for without being preachy or dogmatic. A reporter is much more likely to employ the comments of an advocate who seems thoughtful and concerned rather than one with an obvious agenda that he is trying to force into the article.

Don't Use Foul Language

Most newspapers and television stations won't use a sound bite that is rude. Your interview will likely get left on the cutting-room floor at the station if you don't sound professional.

Do Not Lie or Exaggerate Statistics

Avoid lying, exaggerating statistics, and all other cheaters' tactics. The news media will likely broadcast a colorful statement, but overstating your position sends up a nice softball for your opposition to knock out of the park.

You should not use any statistic that you cannot cite by identifying its source and context. Lying backfires. Don't do it.

Don't Take Personal Shots

Attack your opponent's arguments, not his or her character. It is cowardly to engage in a personal fight through the news media. In a democracy, people are allowed to have different points of view without being vilified in front of the entire community. It is not your job to ruin someone's good name. Rather, your job is to provide a compelling alternative to his or her position on a specific issue.

Don't Attack the Journalist

The reporter, like any other person, will not want to include you in his piece if he feels you are rude and uncivilized to him. Worse yet, he will never, ever call you again when the issue pops up. You want to build the same long-term relationships with the news media that you want to build with your elected officials. It is the job of a reporter to play the devil's advocate and to challenge you on controversial points. Make sure you are emotionally and intellectually prepared to answer challenges to your position on the issues without resorting to personal attacks.

An overly aggressive interview subject also tends to turn off viewers at home, no matter how important or righteous you feel your position is. You will sell more people with confidence evidenced by assured restraint.

Dress Conservatively

You want viewers to focus on your story, not your clothing. Appear professional and serious about your subject matter. Dress as you would for a job interview.

Do Not Ask to Edit the Piece

The reporter is in charge of a news piece and will not allow you to edit or make editorial suggestions. If you do not want something to appear in print, don't say it.

Don't Talk to the News Media If You Don't Want To

A news media request for an interview is not a summons to appear before a judge. It is your decision. If you are not comfortable in front of a camera or feel that your knowledge is not sufficient or your story is too personal, or if you cannot field a few probing questions without flying into a rage, then clearly decline to be interviewed should the news media make a request. If they won't leave you alone, summon the police as you would with any other serious pest, but do not give them any footage of you losing your temper.

Advice from the Field

Kevin Schultze

Reporter

WJLA (ABC affiliate in Washington, D.C.)

"A call to a specific reporter is always better than an anonymous press release. Hundreds of press releases come in every day. There is a lot of competition, and if it is not immediately clear what the local angle is, a press release is easy to ignore. However, if someone calls me and says, 'I have an idea for a story,' or, 'I saw you did a story on this last week, and I wanted to know if you would be interested in an additional angle,' then I begin to have a relationship with that person. I am far more likely to seriously consider the story and to pitch it to my news editors."

HOW TO KNOW IF SOMETHING IS NEWSWORTHY

If you would like to pitch a news story or interview to a particular editor or reporter, it helps if your pitch possesses some of the following newsworthy qualities:

- The story generates compelling images (especially for broadcast news media).
- An elected official or celebrity will be present.
- It is an absolute first.
- You have a personal story of struggle, triumph, or justice.
- You have cultivated a relationship with a news reporter who is interested in repeatedly covering your issue.
- Something has fundamentally changed the nature of your issue.
- It is of legitimate importance to a significant portion of the local population.
- You are available to be interviewed immediately so that reporters can meet their deadlines.
- Your story has been structured to relate to the major news stories of the day.

SHOULD YOU SEND A PRESS RELEASE?

Most advocates want to fax or mail out press releases as a way to let the news media know that they have a local event or an idea for a news story. Press releases are concise, one- to two-page written notices that pitch stories to the news media.

As is the case with so many things, pitching a news story on paper does not convey the power or the urgency that a phone call or in-person meeting with a reporter can have. Press releases arrive at newspapers and television stations by the hundreds, further diminishing their potential impact. Still, if a reporter is interested in a story idea you have, it may help her to have a summary of the event or issue on paper to help her get permission to cover the story from the editor or news director. A well-written press release that includes the logo of your local organization can help establish your credibility as a community expert if the reporter has never met you, so press releases do have their uses. Just be careful. It is a mistake to write a press release and fax it out to hundreds of news media outlets hoping that some of them will bite. In most cases, none will. Your time is much better spent calling a few local reporters whom you know understand or are sympathetic with your issues and directly talking with them to pitch a story idea and then follow up the conversation with a press release so that the reporter has something on paper to share with others in planning meetings.

Internet Tip

To find contact information for your local news media outlets, try NewsLink: newslink.org or NewsDirectory: newsdirectory.com.

IT'S TIME FOR ACTION!

The challenge now belongs to you. Will you take action on the issues you care about?

As you become more sophisticated about the American legislative process and the arguments related to the issues you care about, you may be tempted to gradually replace your individual stories and insights with hard-won erudition, impressive statistics, perhaps a demonstrable comfort with legalese. Be careful. If you dismiss the anecdotal traces of your existence as a human being, you might experience a commensurate diminishing of your effectiveness. The local stories and statistics I encourage you to develop in this book are not place-holders for future substance. They remain the most powerful types of information you can share with your elected officials and the local news media to advance your legislative priorities.

It has been the aim of this book to demonstrate that high-impact grass-roots actions will contribute in a significant way to the legislative process at every level of government. Beyond that, every grassroots action you take resonates beyond a win or lose on a particular issue. Your participation helps our republic sparkle with a multifaceted complexity that confounds the impulse of heartless statisticians and lazy candidates to oversimplify our problems and potential solutions. Your substantive participation helps manifest a dynamic cross-section of our nation and our collective lives, loves, passions, beliefs, hopes, concerns, and ideas. This is the United States at its best, and American democracy within striking distance of its promise.

Ultimately, we are not fighting a series of legislative battles but carrying a torch, the light of which passes beyond the lives of any one of us and along a horizon that describes the longevity of an outrageous political experiment called democracy.

CREATE A CUSTOMIZED TRAINING MANUAL FOR YOUR GRASSROOTS NETWORK!

Is your grassroots network ready to:

- Take action?
- Get mobilized?
- Get results?

The One-Hour Activist is available in volume discounts and can be customized with:

- Your organization's logo on the cover
- A personalized message to your advocates (interior)
- Your legislative agenda, talking points, and voting records (interior)
- Your Web site information

Christopher Kush can train your network in person through special training packages offered with bulk sales.

Help transform each and every one of your advocates into a *One-Hour Activist*.

Please contact specialsales@wiley.com for more information.